Mastering Finance

HSC Business Studies Topic 3

Graham Roll

*This book is dedicated to the late Mike Lembach —
friend, colleague & mentor.*

Five Senses Education Pty Ltd
2/195 Prospect Highway
Seven Hills 2147
New South Wales
Australia

Roll, Graham
Mastering Finance HSC Business Studies Topic 3
ISBN 978-1-74130-982-9

Contents

Rationale

This is a student topic book. Its purpose is to provide a concise, yet comprehensive coverage of the Finance topic in the HSC Course. Students are advised to seek other references and case studies in this topic because it is important to read as widely as possible in order to get the most from your study of the topic.

As far as possible, the material is presented in the same order as the Board of Studies syllabus.

This book includes a syllabus outline with Board of Studies outcomes together with the "learn to" aspects of the topic. Students are reminded that assessment task in Business Studies will always relate to syllabus topics and outcomes.

For case studies, students may find that useful information may be obtained by contacting the various chambers of commerce in addition to government departments and by using the internet which will give you up to date information in this area. Indeed, students who are aiming to maximise their performance in Business Studies should research these web sites and read newspaper articles for the most up to date facts and figures.

Topic 3

FINANCE

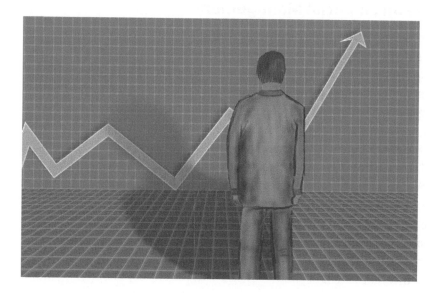

The focus of the topic is the role of interpreting financial information in the planning and management of a business.

Overview of Content and Outcomes

Finance relates to the supply and monitoring of assets, securities and other resources within a business. It is also concerned with how the business interacts with other financial organisations as it deals with those resources.

When considering finance we will examine:
- The role of financial management
- Influences on financial management
- Processes of financial management
- Financial management strategies.

3.1 The Role of Financial Management

- ■ The strategic role of financial management
- ■ The objectives of financial management:
  - – profitability, growth efficiency, liquidity and solvency
  - – short term and long term objectives
  - – interdependence with other key functions of business

3.2 Influences on Financial Management

- ■ Internal sources of finance- retained profits
- ■ External sources of finance such as:
  - – debt, short-term borrowing (overdraft, commercial bills, factoring), long-term borrowing (mortgage, debentures, unsecured notes, leasing)
  - – equity, ordinary shares (new issues, rights issues, placements, share purchase plans), private equity
- ■ Financial institutions: banks, investment banks, finance companies, superannuation funds, life insurance companies, unit trusts and the Australian Securities Exchange
- ■ Influence of government: Australian Securities and Investment Commission, company taxation
- ■ Global market influences such as the economic outlook, availability of funds and interest rates.

3.3 Processes of Financial Management

- ■ Planning and implementing - financial needs, budgets, record systems, financial risks and financial controls
  - – debt and equity financing and the advantages and disadvantages of each
  - – matching the terms and source of finance to business purpose
  - – Monitoring and controlling - the cash flow statement, income statement and balance sheet
  - – Financial ratios
  - – liquidity i.e. current ratio (current assets/current liabilities)
  - – Gearing i.e. debt to equity ratio (total liabilities/total equity)
  - – profitability i.e. gross profit ratio (gross profit/sales); net profit ratio (net profit/sales); return on equity ratio (net profit/total equity)
  - – efficiency i.e. expense ratio (total expenses/sales); accounts receivable turnover ratio (sales/accounts receivable)
  - – comparative ratio analysis - over different periods of time, against common standards and with similar businesses
- ■ Limitations of financial reports - normalised earnings, capitalising expenses, valuing assets, timing issues, debt repayments, notes to the financial statements
- ■ Ethical issues related to financial reports

3.4 Financial Management Strategies

- Cash flow management:
  - cash flow statements
  - distribution of payments, discounts for early payment, factoring
  - Working capital management
  - control of current assets (cash receivables, inventories)
  - control of current liabilities (payable, loans, overdrafts)
  - strategies (leasing, sale and lease back)
- Profitability management:
  - cost controls (fixed and variable, cost centres, expense minimisation)
  - revenue controls and marketing objectives
- Global financial management:
  - exchange rates
  - interest rates
  - methods of international payment such as payment in advance, letter of credit, clean payment and bill of exchange
  - hedging
  - derivatives

Outcomes

The 9 outcomes for this topic are to:

- ▪ evaluate management strategies in response to changes in internal and external influences
- ▪ discuss the social and ethical responsibilities of management
- ▪ analyse business functions and processes in large global businesses
- ▪ explain management strategies and their impact on business
- ▪ evaluate the effectiveness of management in the performance of business
- ▪ plan and conduct investigations into contemporary business practices
- ▪ organise and evaluate information for actual and hypothetical business situations
- ▪ communicate business information, issues and concepts in appropriate formats
- ▪ apply mathematical concepts appropriately in business situations.

Also important to the understanding of your syllabus content is the section of the syllabus known as the "learn to" components of the topic. Here you are being asked to examine contemporary business issues in order to be able to:

- ▪ Explain the potential conflicts between short-term and long-term financial objectives
- ▪ Analyse the influence of government and the global market on financial management
- ▪ Identify the limitations of financial reporting
- ▪ Compare the risks involved in domestic and global financial transactions

You are also being asked to investigate aspects of business using hypothetical situations and actual business case studies to:

- ▪ calculate key financial ratios
- ▪ assess business performance using comparative ratio analysis
- ▪ recommend strategies to improve financial performance
- ▪ examine ethical financial reporting practices.

3.1 The Role Of Financial Management

The strategic role of financial management

Finance managers in a business control:

- the flow of funds
- record keeping
- compliance with legal regulations
- planning future funds needs and
- aquisition of financial resources.

They are responsible not only for the day to day management of these funds but are also required to consider long term implications. A strategic role infers that the management and planning is undertaken over a 3 to 5 years time span.

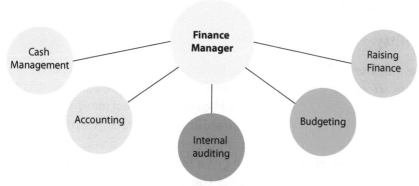

Financial Structure - Medium Sized Business

To assist with strategic financial management the business must develop budgets. These are quantitative forecasts that help guide the use of the financial inputs and outgoings of a business. They perform an important planning function. They set desired financial targets and these targets can be measured against actual performance i.e. they set out the anticipated financial needs of the business over a period of time. The two main financial budgets are cash flow and capital expenditure budgets.

- Cash flow budgets predict the flow of funds into and out of a business over a period of time. They are used to inform management about their financial obligations in running the business.
- Capital expenditure budgets assists management to control capital equipment spending without limiting current expenditure obligations.

Apart from the development of budgets to assist in strategic planning, a business must consider the financial needs of the business in terms of planning for the following:

- taxation obligations
- risk management through insurance
- credit control
- short and long term investing
- short and long term borrowing
- controlling cash flow
- raising finance for expansion

Thus, the strategic role of financial management cannot be underestimated with regard to the planning options of the business.

Objectives of financial management

The main financial objectives of a business are concerned with:

- maximising profits
- facilitating growth
- improving efficiency
- maintaining liquidity and
- remaining solvent.

Profitability

This refers to the yield or profit a business receives in return for its productive effort. Profitability is an important objective because it is the level of profitability that determines the level of investment funds that can be attracted to a business. Poor profitability can have a detrimental effect on the share price of a business and its ability to pay dividends to shareholders. It is a good indicator of the wellbeing of a business and the efficiency with which it is being managed. It also tells the owners/managers that the products and services that the business is delivering are the correct ones, priced appropriately and marketed correctly.

> **Focus Point**
>
> *Profitability is a good indicator of the wellbeing of a business and the efficiency with which it is being managed.*

Growth

Most, but not all businesses in Australia have the objective of trying to grow into a larger operation. Businesses tend to grow financially and physically. Growth is achieved in three broad ways:

- **Firstly,** by increasing sales and therefore by expanding its operations. Often new branches are opened throughout the city, interstate or even internationally.
- **Secondly,** by merging with or acquiring other businesses. This method of growth is common with the business in question merging with or acquiring a competing business.
- **Thirdly,** a business may diversify into other areas unrelated to the original business. For example, a chemical company may diversify into the manufacture of computers. In the balance sheet, growth is measured by the growth in the value of the business assets.

Efficiency

Efficiency describes how well a business is being run i.e. how efficiently the business is using its resources such as labour, finance or equipment and in particular collecting its debts. If a business is able to get more out of its labour resources for the same cost, then the business has increased its efficiency. For a period of time the main way of increasing efficiency in the area of labour was to downsize but this has now been largely disregarded as a method of increasing efficiency. Now many businesses are looking to improve their levels of training rather than necessarily downsizing.

Other inputs may be finances or equipment and in the same way there must be managed efficiently. For example, the business must adopt the most efficient method of obtaining finance. This may be the various forms of debt or equity financing (or a combination of both). In terms of equipment, the latest technology needs to be used particularly with computer aided technology.

It should be noted that much of the efficiency we refer to in this context relates to financial efficiency, because all things being equal, if the business is being run efficiently then financial returns will be maximised.

Liquidity

This is the ability of a business to pay its short term obligations as they fall due. All businesses should have the objective of being liquid. Indeed if a business cannot pay its short term obligations then it is said to be insolvent and is the prime cause of a business failing. This is because if a business cannot pay its phone bills, power bills, rent or wages etc it will be out of business in weeks. The phone and power will be cut off, the landlord will change the locks and employees will resign if they are not being paid. In addition if a business cannot remain liquid and cannot pay its short term debts then it can be wound up by a court order through a request of its creditors.

> **Focus Point**
>
> *The first financial goal is to remain liquid. Liquidity is the ability of a business to pay its short term obligations as they fall due.*

Liquid assets take the form of cash at bank, stock if it is readily converted into cash, plus any other assets that can be converted into cash in a short period of time. Liquidity is also affected by the amount of current liabilities that a business has i.e. items such as overdrafts, accounts payable and short term credit obtained by the business which must be paid back in a very short period of time. A balance sheet will show the liquidity of a business described as current assets minus current liabilities. (This will be demonstrated later in the book.)

There are several factors which determine how liquid a business needs to be. For example, if a business sells its goods for cash, then it doesn't need to hold very much in the form of cash assets. However, if there is a long lead time between the sale of the product or delivery of service and payment, then the business needs to hold a higher proportion of its assets in liquid cash form.

To be liquid a business needs to have at least $1 of liquid current assets for every $1 of current liabilities- giving a ratio of current assets to current liabilities of 1:1. Ideally though the ratio should be greater than 1:1 and even up to 2:1 in cases where cash flow is irregular.

Solvency

Solvency can be described as the state in which a business is capable of paying all its debts as they arise or fall due. Solvency also refers to the ability of a business to meet its long term commitments such as a mortgage. Most businesses need to borrow money in the normal course of events to expand and this is a healthy and normal thing. However, a business that relies too heavily on borrowed funds is said to be highly geared.

A company which continues to trade when it is unable to pay its debts can be a personal liability on its directors and there are certain rules, regulations and steps that have to be followed as the table on page 171 shows.

Insolvent businesses close down.

The following information was taken from the ACCC Website:

Is my company in financial difficulty?

Signs that may indicate your company is in financial difficulty include ongoing losses, poor cash flow, unpaid creditors outside usual trading terms and problems obtaining finance.

If you receive a penalty notice from the Commissioner of Taxation for your company's unpaid tax, you should immediately seek professional advice. Failure to take appropriate steps within 14 days may result in the Commissioner taking recovery action against you personally for an amount equivalent to the unpaid tax.

What do I do if my company is in financial difficulty?

If you suspect your company is in financial difficulty, get proper accounting and legal advice as early as possible, as this increases the likelihood of the company surviving.

What if my company is insolvent?

If your company is insolvent, do not allow it to incur further debt. Unless it is possible to promptly restructure, refinance or obtain equity funding to recapitalise the company, generally, your options are to appoint a voluntary administrator or a liquidator. The three most common insolvency procedures are voluntary administration, liquidation and receivership. (This was dealt with in the preliminary course)

What are my duties as a director?

If your company is insolvent, or there is a real risk of insolvency, your duties as a director are expanded to include the interests of creditors (including employees and other stakeholders). As well as general directors' duties, you also have a duty to prevent your company trading if it is insolvent.

What are the consequences of insolvent trading?

Insolvent trading can have serious consequences for directors. There are various penalties associated with insolvent trading, including civil penalties, compensation proceedings and criminal charges.

How does an external administration affect me as a director?

There are a number of consequences for directors of a company that goes into external administration. These vary depending on the type of external administration.

What is my role in assisting an external administrator?

As a company officer, you must assist any external administrator (e.g. liquidator, receiver, administrator) who has been appointed to your company. You must provide reports as to affairs (commonly known as RATAs), records, information and other assistance.

Case Study

Court Investigation of Insolvency

The Case

The recent decision of Austin Australia Pty Ltd v De Martin Gasparini Pty Ltd [2007] NSWSC 1238 considered the definition of, and tests for determining, "solvency" under the Corporations Act 2001 (Cth).

The case was part of a preference proceeding, that dealt with the winding up of a corporation, Austin Australia Pty Ltd (Austin). It was necessary for the court to answer as a separate question whether Austin was "insolvent" under the statutory meaning during the period 30 June 2003 and 31 December 2003.

In deciding the question of solvency, the court had regard to the following evidence:

- Available cash flow as evidenced by bank statements and the amount owing by the prior month's debtors. Deductions were made for unpresented cheques, retentions and provisions.
- Cash flow showed Austin did not have enough cash on a month-by-month basis to cover its accounts due and payable from March 2003 to November 2003. A deficit ran from $3 million in June 2003 to $7.3 million in November 2003.
- In November 2003, there were between 600 and 700 unpresented cheques, totalling $7,891,004.08. $1,181,981.28 of this figure had been released to payees, but were unpaid at month's end. $6,709,022.80 were cheques drawn but not released to payees. It was inferred that these cheques were deliberately held back.
- Austin's debtors that had been outstanding for over 120 days increased from 4% to 22% from April 2003 to November 2003. It was considered unlikely that these debts would be recovered in full.
- "Cash burn" exceeded available cash for each of January, March, April, May, September, October and December 2003.
- There was a total accumulated loss of $1,413,020 from November 2002 to November 2003, without write offs for bad debts, doubtful debts or other adjustments.
- Austin also had proceedings against debtors in the New South Wales Court of Appeal, the Magistrates' Court of Queensland, the District Court at Penrith, the Local Court at Orange, the Local Court at Parramatta, the District Court at Sydney and the Melbourne Magistrates' Court.

The decision of Barrett J

Barrett J found Austin's position was not merely a temporary situation. Profitability did not exist and the company could not meet its debts. Further, there were no external sources of funds for it to draw on. This resulted in the finding that there was an endemic shortage of working capital and inability to pay debts, and that the company was insolvent from 30 June 2003 to 31 December 2003. *(Article from the Corrs Chambers Westgarth Website "Making Business Sense")*

Short-term and long-term goals

In the short term, the most important financial goal for a business is to remain liquid. Staying liquid enables a business to remain open and trading. In the longer term, the business wants to begin to make a profit and grow. Initially, many businesses don't make a profit and may even make a loss.

The first few years' revenue may be used to pay down loans and establishment costs. New business owners often work for no wages, preferring to build up a sound business, and preserve working capital.

In the longer term, once the business is established owners can start to pay themselves a greater share of the profits.

Long term goals will include:
- growth
- profitability
- efficiency
- solvency.

Focus Point

The longer term objectives include profitability, solvency, efficiency & growth.

Interdependence with other key business functions

In the Preliminary Course you will have studied the "key business functions" of operations, marketing, finance and human resources. Indeed the HSC Course revolves around these four key business functions.

The study of this course should indicate to you that a business doesn't operate in little compartments of separate functions. Each of these functions are interdependent upon each other.

For example, the operations function requires a financial input or budget so that management can cost its inputs into the business such as raw materials, facilities and human resources, cost its transformational processes such as technology requirements and monitoring costs and its outputs such as warranties and customer service etc.

In other words inputs, transformational processes and outputs cost money and they have to be budgeted and accounted for. The finance section of the business must advise the operations manager about costing budgets and spending priorities.

In terms of the marketing of the good or service, as with operations above a marketing budget has to be made so that marketing costs don't blow out and that the right amount of money is spent marketing the product to the customer otherwise efficiency levels will fall.

Human resources have to be budgeted for and costed, especially since the cost of labour (human resources) is often one of the largest expenses for businesses/a business. Many businesses will pay top dollars to get the right personnel in key areas of the business because they will return high levels of profit to the business if they have the skills and personality. Even at lower levels within the business, staffing numbers can have an important bearing on the profitability of a business.

REVISION EXERCISES 3.1

1. Define the term 'strategic financial management' and explain what it involves.

_____

_____

_____

_____

2. What is a budget? Describe the **two** types of financial budget.

_____

_____

_____

_____

3. Apart from budgets, list the **seven** items that business managers must consider in terms of financial management.

_____

_____

_____

_____

4. Explain the broad objectives of financial management listed below.

   a. Profitability

   _____

   b. Growth

   _____

   c. Efficiency

   _____

   d. Liquidity

   _____

   e. Solvency

   _____

REVISION EXERCISES 3.1

5. Explain the short-term and long-term goals of financial management.

_____

_____

_____

_____

_____

_____

_____

_____

6. Explain how financial management is interdependent with the other key business functions.

_____

_____

_____

_____

_____

_____

_____

_____

_____

_____

_____

_____

_____

3.2 Influences on Financial Management

Finance managers have three main devices available to them to monitor and control assets, liabilities, income and expenditure. These are a **Cash Flow Report**, an **Income Statement**, and a **Balance Sheet**.

The Balance Sheet is a snapshot of the assets, liabilities and equities at a particular point of time, typically calculated at the end of the financial year. The diagram below shows where typical balance sheet items occur on a balance sheet.

Assets

Current Assets
- Cash
- Shares
- Inventories
- Accounts Receivable

Long Term Assets
- Plant and Equipment
- Real Estate
- Investments
- Furniture and Fittings
- Motor Vehicles
- Superannuation Funds
- Infrastructure
- Corporate assets
- Long term inventory

=

Liabilities

Short Term Borrowings
- Overdraft
- Commercial Bills
- Factoring
- Accounts Payable

Long Term Borrowings
- Mortgage
- Debentures
- Unsecured Notes
- Leasing

+

Equities

Owner's Equity
- Share Capital
- Retained earnings
- Reserves

Private Equity

When a business expands it needs to acquire additional funds. Expansion increases the assets under management in a business or converts short term assets (cash etc) to long term assets (e.g. equipment or real estate).

If additional funds are acquired, they will come from:
- external sources (increases in short term and long term borrowings, or selling more shares).
- internal sources (using up reserves or retained earnings).

Internal sources of finance

Retained profits

When a business makes a profit, some of the money is paid to owners and shareholders as dividends. The balance not distributed is retained by the business to continue the operations of the business or purchase new capital equipment. How much is retained will vary according to the circumstances and size of the business. The proportion of profits retained by the business depends on a number of factors:

- the need for funds to undertake expansion
- the expectation of shareholders concerning dividend policy
- the cash flow needs of the business to take account of seasonal fluctuations.

Retained profits are regarded as the main internal source of finance.

Reserves

Reserves may be a possible source of funds if:

- the business operates more efficiently by reducing inventories
- account managers ensure receivables are collected on time (generating more cash)
- cash resources are applied more effectively
- expendure on raw materials is carried out more economically (reducing payables).

A cash surplus generated by these actions may be applied to funding the expansion of the business.

External sources of finance

Where a business is unable to meet its demand for finance internally, it is necessary to look outside the business. External sources of funds can be:

- **Short Term Borrowing** (overdraft, commercial bills, factoring)
- **Long Term Borrowing** (mortgage, debentures, unsecured notes, leasing)
- **Equity** shares (new issues, rights issues, placements, share purchase plans) and private equity.

Short-term borrowing

This is made up of overdrafts and commercial bills and is normally used when the business requires finance for a relatively short time of up to a year or when the finance is required to assist with working capital.

This situation might arise when a business requires working capital (funds) on setting up of the business or at peak times such as Christmas to pay for stock. In another situation a business might require short-term finances in order to fund a project that will give financial results in a short period of time.

Overdrafts

An overdraft is an agreement between a bank and a business allowing the business to overdraw on its cheque account up to a certain, agreed figure. The bank charges interest and fees on the overdraft amount. This is the most common type of short-term financing because it is very flexible. The bank will not normally require the business to repay the overdraft, therefore the business can use the facility as a permanent line of credit if it wishes to do so. This is particularly helpful when the business requires extra cash flow to pay unexpected bills or take advantage of purchasing some cheap stock that may have become available.

Usually the bank will extend an overdraft to any business it thinks is credit worthy, but occasionally it may require some form of asset security. This will allow the bank to sell the asset to retrieve its overdraft should the business default on its overdraft.

Commercial bills

These are known as bills of exchange. They are a promise to pay a certain sum of money say in 30, 60 or 90 days time if a business requires it, for example to pay for stock that they know they can sell very quickly. The bank doesn't actually supply the funds but provides their credit rating for the business.

Factoring

This is the selling of accounts receivable to a financier. This is regarded as an important source of finance because the business is receiving immediate funds to use as working capital. It works this way: a business sells its accounts receivable to a factoring company at a discount rate. The factoring company then collects those accounts receivable. The difference between the figure that the accounts receivable were for and what they are collected for is the profit taken by the factoring company. For example, if a business has $100,000 worth of accounts receivable that are difficult to collect, it may sell those accounts for say $95,000. Even though the business doesn't get all of its money, it receives most of it immediately rather than having to write off the debt i.e. the business doesn't receive the money at all. The firm can now continue on with its business. In the mean time the factoring company collects the accounts receivable taking $5,000 profit.

Long-term borrowing

Borrowings that are not required to be repaid in current terms are called long term. These include:

- mortgages
- debentures
- unsecured notes
- leasing
- commercial hire purchase arrangements.

Long term borrowing is primarily used to fund long term assets. A business will increase long term borrowings to expand business activities such as setting up a new operation interstate or simply extending existing premises. It may also be used to finance the takeover of a competitor. The time scale relating to long term borrowing may be from 1-2 years up to 15-20 years.

Mortgages

This is a loan giving the lender first claim over specified assets such as land or buildings which are used as security. Mortgages are normally used to purchase a business or premises. A business may use mortgage funds for approved reasons such as the purchase of capital equipment.

A **chattel** mortgage is a mortgage where the security is taken over non-property assets owned by the business. With any mortgage, the mortgagor (lender) is able to seize the assets on default- if the mortgagee (borrower) is unable to repay the funds. Chattel mortgages are not very common or popular in Australia, most lenders preferring to use property as security. If an asset is mortgaged, the borrower (business) is unable to sell any of those assets without the permission of the lender.

Debentures

A debenture is a loan to a company that is usually secured. The security here tends to be on the overall assets of the business rather than the land and buildings as with a mortgage. The debenture allows the business to use the funds supplied by the lenders for a specific period of time, after which the loan must be paid back plus interest. The lender relies on his assessment that the borrower will pay the agreed interest and that the loan will be repaid at the end of the term.

The details of the loan are outlined in a prospectus outlining the conditions of the loan. The prospectus will contain information about:

- reasons why the business is seeking funds
- interest rates to be paid
- frequency of dividends and
- maturity date i.e. when they will get their money back.

In this way the potential lender is aware of the conditions attached to the loan.

Unsecured notes

An unsecured note is also a loan to a company that is not secured.
These notes often rank behind debentures if funds for repayment are in
short supply. They usually pay a higher than normal rate of interest return.
They are usually only issued by companies of high reputation and status with
a sound financial record. By unsecured we mean that if the business who has
borrowed the money goes broke, the lenders (usually the general public) will
be last in line to get their money back. Unsecured notes are usually issued for
periods ranging from three months to three years.

Below are some of the key features of an unsecured note issue (issued by
Mackay Sugar Limited in 2010 designed to raise finance from members
of the public). The funds were probably needed to finance the purchase of
sugar cane from growers. The funds enable the mill to process the crop and
subsequently sell the refined product, recoup the money and repay the notes
with interest. The use of unsecured notes is quite common where a business
needs to fund seasonal activities.

Key features of the Unsecured Notes
Issuer Mackay Sugar Limited ACN 057 463 671.
Issue price per Unsecured Note $1.
Minimum investment*: There is no minimum investment amount for
7 Day Call Unsecured Notes. The minimum investment is $1,000 for each
purchase of the Selected Term Unsecured Note or 6, 12 and 24 Months.*
Maximum investment: *There is no maximum investment amount for
Unsecured Notes.*
Interest rate: *Interest accumulates from the Date of Investment.*
Calculation of interest*: The interest payable on the Unsecured Notes is
calculated daily from the date of investment.*
Payment of interest: *Mackay Sugar will use its best endeavours to
ensure that interest payments are made to Noteholders within 14 days
after the interest becomes payable. Unless otherwise designated on the
Application or Rate Sheet, all periodic interest payments on the Unsecured
Notes will be invested in 7 Day Call Unsecured Notes.*
No security: *The Unsecured Notes are unsecured and are not guaranteed
by any party. In the event of a winding-up of Mackay Sugar, Noteholders will
rank for payment behind secured creditors (including NAB and Rabobank).
Requests for redemption: A request for the 7 Day Call Unsecured Notes to
be redeemed may be made at any time with the delivery of written notice
to Mackay Sugar. For Selected Term Unsecured Notes and for the 6, 12 or
24 Month Unsecured Notes, the Noteholder must deliver written notice to
Mackay Sugar advising that they wish to redeem the Unsecured Notes at
least ten Business Days prior to the Maturity Date.
Rollover: If no instructions are received by Mackay Sugar then the Maturing
Money will be invested in new Unsecured Notes for the same term and at the
interest rate listed in the current Rate Sheet and the interest payable on
the Maturing Money will be invested in 7 Day Call Unsecured Notes.*

Leasing

This is an agreement where the owner of an asset (lessor) allows the use of that asset by a lessee for a periodic charge. In practical terms, a lease agreement is the same as a rental agreement. The user does not own the asset, but pays a regular amount to use the asset. Lease payments are an expense incurred by a business and are thus deductible from income for taxation purposes.

Leasing is regarded as a long-term source of finance. When a business leases equipment they are not using up their working capital which can then be used for other purposes in the business.

Common items leased by business include motor vehicles and office equipment, although any business asset may be leased. The business enters into a contract with the leasing company outlining the details of the lease which usually includes service of the equipment as part of the deal.

There are two types of leases - operating leases and financial leases.

- **Operating leases:** The business rents the asset for an agreed period and returns it to the lender (bank or finance company) at the end of the term. There is usually no obligation or opportunity to purchase the asset at the end of the lease period. Lease payments are tax deductible.
- **Financial leases:** Here the business makes tax deductible lease payments for the period of the lease; the lessee has the option to purchase the item for a residual price at the end of the term. The final payment is regarded as a capital purchase because the ownership of the asset passes from the finance company to the business.

HOW LEASING WORKS

- The lessee (customer or borrower) will select an asset.
- The lessor (finance company) will purchase that asset.
- The lessee will have use of that asset during the lease.
- The lessee will pay a series of rentals for the use of that asset.
- The lessor will recover a large part or all of the cost of the asset earn interest from the rentals paid by the lessee.
- The lessee has the option to acquire ownership of the asset.

As a source of finance, leasing is attractive because:
- there are no large initial cash outlays so working capital is conserved
- leasing is convenient and flexible
- costs are known on a monthly basis which helps cash flow
- lease finance may provide 100% of required funds
- lease payments are tax deductible.

Establishing a Business

When a business is first established, shares are sold to those wanting to invest in the business. These funds come from shareholder's personal savings or assets they may be able to access. Apart from a small business owner who simply puts his/her own money into the business, medium to larger businesses issue **shares** as a way of raising finance for start-up.

Most businesses issue **ordinary shares.** These are shares issued to investors in companies that entitle purchasers (holders) to a part ownership of the business. It entitles them to receive dividends or bonus shares when they are issued from time-to-time. These shares can be traded on the Australian Securities Exchange (ASX). Share capital is made up of the money that individuals have paid into the business to be part owners of that business.

Equity

Equity refers to the capital and accumulated funds and reserves shown in the balance sheet. **Owners equity** includes the funds contributed by shareholders, and retained profits not paid as dividends. **Private equity** derives from external sources such as merchant banks, retail banks or friends of the business.

Business acquires funds from equity by:
- selling ordinary shares (new issues, rights issues, share placements and share purchase plans)
- private equity (venture capital and leveraged buyouts).

Ordinary shares

An ordinary share represents equity ownership in a company. A shareholder is entitled to vote at a shareholders meeting. The number of shares held determines the voting rights. Shareholders receive income from shares in the form of dividends. If the company is wound up, the assets are distributed in proportion to the shares held, after all debts are paid (discharged). As such, ordinary shareholders are considered unsecured creditors.

Ordinary shares include those traded privately as well as shares that trade on the various public securities exchanges. The true value of an ordinary share is based on:
- the price obtained through market forces
- the value of the underlying business
- investor sentiment toward the company.

New Share Issues

When a private or public company wishes to raise more capital it undertakes a new issue of shares. For a proprietary company, new shares can be issued to existing shareholders or new shareholders if there are fewer than 50 of them. However the company directors must adhere to strict rules and regulations set down by ASIC for this to happen.

A public company must also register with ASIC to actually enable it to issue new shares. When issuing shares it must be accompanied by a prospectus. A prospectus is required by ASIC when the company seeks to issue new shares to the public. This prospectus must include:

- the latest audited financial statements
- forecasts for the business
- what the funds will be used for and
- an accountants report on the reliability of the information contained in the prospectus.

This then gives potential investors a good idea about the business and how financially secure it is. Issues are possible without a prospectus in some circumstances (see **Share Placements** at the bottom of this page).

Rights issues

A company may choose to raise new funds by offering additional shares to existing shareholders. Shares are offered in proportion to existing shareholdings. These offers giving the 'right' to buy new shares are called 'rights issues'

Rights issues are often made at a discount on the market price. A rights issue might be "one for two". This means that for every two shares held, each shareholder has the right to buy another share. In this situation, if you own 200 shares, you are being offered the opportunity to take up to 100 new shares. A shareholder may take up all, some or none of the offer. Sometimes it is permissible to sell rights on the securities market, enabling others to buy the shares.

Share placements

Companies may raise money through **share placements,** where companies listed on the **ASX** are offered shares at a discount. Such issues are made:

- without seeking shareholder approval and
- without a formal prospectus.

Normal retail shareholders are excluded, diluting their rights of ownership. Institutional investors and large corporations increase their ownership and control by this preferential access to share purchase.

Without share placements, companies have sometimes struggled to raise money through the traditional sources. As the Australian share market has grown, companies have found institutional and large investors willing to come up with extra capital, often in large amounts, within 24 hours. Generally, institutional and large investors invest at least $500,000 at a time. Many companies believe the speed and cost savings make placements a better choice than a traditional rights issue.

Offers are made to ASX listed investors without a prospectus because they are regarded as experienced: offers to retail investors require a prospectus to protect them from the risks of uninformed investment.

Share purchase plans

ASIC has issued a document, Regulatory Guide 125, which sets out the conditions for the operation of Share Purchase Plans. The first two paragraphs in the guide precisely define the scope of the plans.

Share purchase plans
RG 125.1 *A share purchase plan is a plan for the offer to existing investors of shares by a company listed on the Australian Securities Exchange (ASX).*
RG 125.2 *Share purchase plans give existing members a convenient means of obtaining additional shares that are priced at a discount to the market price during a particular period before the offer and without brokerage fees or stamp duty.*

Share Purchase Plans operate similarly to share placements. The main difference is that the shares are only offered to existing shareholders of the issuing company rather than to the larger group of ASX listed investors.

Share purchase plans are restricted by ASIC to an annual limit of $15000 per shareholder (since 2009). They are an efficient device used by listed companies to raise funds from their members(shareholders), without incurring the usual costs of printing offer documents and prospectuses. The investors benefit by the provisions of RG125.2 enabling them to buy shares at a discount.

Private Equity

Investment banks provide a mechanism for professional investors to place funds in start-up businesses who may otherwise not have access to funds.

Private equity investment is also available for:
- a venture capital firm (firm concentrating on new businesses)
- an angel investor (rich investors who are attracted to the recipient company aims and objectives).

Each of these investors provide working capital to a target company to either nuture their expansion, assist in new product development, or enable the restructuring of the company's ownership, operations or management. Private equity funds are often withdrawn after the new venture matures into an operational strategy. Sometimes the private equity investors morph into normal shareholders.

The most common investment strategies adopted by private equity investors are:
- leveraged buyouts (to enable a takeover of the business)
- venture capital (for bringing new ideas into commercial reality)
- growth capital (to enable the business to develop)
- distressed investments (to enable an investment project to be restarted)
- mezzanine finance (Preferential equity funds ranking before shareholder dividends in the company structure.)

A critique of share placements

Share placements must be banned by legislation

by: Terry McCrann from: *The Australian* April 10, 2010

Corporate Australia is congenitally unable to clean up its act. The prime regulator is institutionally incapable of understanding the inherent corruption. So there is only one course: share placements must be banned by specific legislation. At the moment we not only allow discretionary placements (they should more accurately be termed discriminatory as they steal money from retail shareholders) but everything in our corporate system actively encourages them. And I do mean everything. Boards of directors love them. It gives them immediate, painless access to new equity capital.

Investment bankers don't just love them but positively wallow in them. It enables them to get paid millions of dollars for handing out free money, with some of the dollars coming from the very shareholders being plundered. And they are a godsend to institutional investors. Placements below market prices (they are all below market) enable subscribers to record above-market gains, and so underwrite or boost the fees they charge their investors. In a sense, they're bilking retail investors twice over.

Free trial

Further, both the regulator, the Australian Securities & Investments Commission, and the underlying corporate legislation actually encourage them and discourage the fair, sensible alternative: renounceable pro-rata rights issues. All this makes an utter mockery of the claims that the legislation is aimed at ensuring all shareholders in public companies are treated equally, and that ASIC is there to protect investors. Last year, corporate Australia embarked on an absolute orgy (there really is no other word for it) of placements and their barely more equitable sibling, institutional entitlement issues.

They were the primary mechanism for raising well over $100 billion of new equity. That was easily the most raised for any country in the world in, if you'll pardon the irony, pro-rata terms. It was even in the top two or three in absolute dollar terms, although there was one extraordinary exception. Like Kevin and Ken's "stimulus", this orgy of raisings was hailed as a triumph. Stimuluses supposedly kept us out of recession. Never mind the cost. All that equity supposedly allowed corporate Australia to sail through the great deleveraging to the benefit of all their shareholders.

OK, so some institutional and investment banking snouts-in-the-trough benefited, Animal Farm-style, more than the other pigs. But that's the price small shareholders (sorry we all) had to pay. All boats were lifted, so to speak; it's just that some got lifted more. And if it kept the payments going on the holiday spread or boutique vineyard, well, that was even more to the good. The one great exception, rather than proving the rule, utterly destroyed this farrago of self-interested and ignorant nonsense. Rio Tinto raised almost $20bn with a terribly gouache pro-rata renounceable rights issue. And why did it go down such a terribly unfashionable route? Because it had to. Because the rules of the stock exchange mandated it. That's the London Stock Exchange, not the ASX.

Rio showed precisely what was so wrong with the down under placements/entitlement issues. In the fear and loathing of the global financial meltdown, they all had to be done at huge discounts to market. With Rio, and with Rio alone, it didn't matter how big the discount was because the cheap shares went to all shareholders proportionately. If they didn't want to take up their rights, they were sold and non-subscribers were fairly compensated for the dilution.

The non-subscribing retail investors in all other down under placements got nothing to compensate for their dilution. And they were well and truly diluted. Real dollars were taken from their pockets and handed to institutions, even though share prices generally rose in the recovery. Now it is reasonable to argue that directors were acting in the best interests of their companies and, as such, all their shareholders. Survival took precedence over equity. It would have been negligent not to raise equity in that manner.

Except that such a rationalisation misses the point. The reason companies went down the placement/entitlement route is that the whole system has promoted those means of raising equity. And this institutional practice is actively encouraged by both the law and the regulator. This is done by making rights issues cumbersome and untimely and through the use of seductive, seemingly equity-creating follow-on SPPs (small shareholder "share purchase plans") to validate placements/entitlement issues. SPPs do nothing of the sort. They are a further, quite insidious turning of the inequity screw.

They are another layer of non pro-rata uncompensated dilution for many retail shareholders and they opened the door to unscrupulous main-chancers to join the very profitable wallowing. Now the storm has passed, one might have hoped that companies would start treating shareholders fairly. Mirvac has swiftly put paid to that hope. It announced it had raised $350 million from a placement to "existing and new" institutional investors and would follow with a $150m SPP to retail shareholders. Now, true, as the discount to market was relatively small at around 5 per cent to 7 per cent, the amount stolen from its retail holders wasn't large. But Merrill Lynch and UBS were still paid millions to hand out free money.

Clearly, the saying "physician heal thyself"' has no meaning in corporate Australia. Although true, it's a little harder to do in the legislative/regulatory environment. The "healing" has to be "assisted" by changing the law, making renounceable pro-rata rights issues mandatory and banning placements and institutional entitlement issues. This also requires dumping the ludicrous and completely useless prospectus rules that make rights issues so clunky. Are we going to learn any lessons from the meltdown? Probably not. But this one is a no-brainer. If we had had the right, pardon the pun, system in place, we could have still raised that $100bn. But we'd have done it fairly, without stealing from retail investors and handing quite literally billions of dollars to institutional investors, investment bankers and assorted main-chancing flotsam and jetsam.

Financial institutions

When raising additional capital, business may deal with:
- banks
- investment banks
- finance companies
- superannuation funds
- life insurance companies
- unit trusts
- The Australian Securities Exchange (ASX).

Banks

Retail banking services

As a group, banks are by far the largest financial providers in Australia. Even if some businesses don't use banks as a source of funds, all use the services of banks to help them carry out their transactions. They hold deposits, supply cash and provide credit card and cheque account facilities. These services, provided mainly for individuals and small business, are known as retail banking services.

Wholesale banking services

Banks also provide other services, mainly for larger business and government. These include trading packages, foreign exchange, operations between merchant banks and other financial institutions, high value transactions and more sophisticated corporate finance.

Banks in Australia

There are many banks operating in Australia including:
- Adelaide Bank Limited
- AMP Bank Limited
- Australia and New Zealand Banking Group Limited
- Bank of Queensland Limited
- Bendigo Bank Limited
- Colonial State Bank *(the trading name of State Bank of New South Wales Limited)*
- Commonwealth Bank of Australia
- Commonwealth Development Bank of Australia Limited *(a subsidiary of Commonwealth Bank of Australia)*
- Elders Rural Bank
- Macquarie Bank Limited
- National Australia Bank Limited
- St. George Bank Limited
- Suncorp-Metway Limited
- Westpac Banking Corporation.

In addition there are many foreign owned banks operating in Australia at the present time, all of whom provide the similar services as the Australian banks. The introduction of these foreign banks into the Australian banking market was designed to increase competition for providing financial.

Investment banks

An investment bank is a financial institution that assists individuals, corporations and governments in raising capital by acting as the client's agent. The bank helps investors purchase securities, enabling the business to acquire additional funds. An investment bank may also assist companies involved in mergers and acquisitions, and provide ancillary services such as information on market situations.

Unlike retail banks, investment banks do not take deposits. In Australia there has traditionally been a separation between investment banking and retail banking. Other industrialised countries, including G8 countries, have historically not maintained such a separation.

Investment banks offer services to both corporations and investors. Other activities that an investment bank may be involved in include:

- **Global transaction banking** providing cash management, custody services, lending, and securities brokerage services to institutions.
- **Investment management** is the professional management of shares and bonds etc. and other assets such as real estate. Investors may be institutions such as insurance companies, pension funds and corporations etc or private investors.
- **Risk management** involving analysing the market and credit risk that traders are taking onto the balance sheet in conducting their daily trades. Risk managers limit the amount of capital traded to prevent "bad" trades having a detrimental effect on the business.
- **Financial control** tracking and analysing the capital flows of the firm , limiting unwise decisions.
- **Corporate strategy** planning.
- ensuring **Compliance with government regulations.**

Investment banks operating in Australia include:

- JP Morgan
- Deutsche bank
- Credit Suisse
- Macquarie Group Limited
- CommSec
- Goldman Sachs
- Barclays
- BNP Paribas
- HSBC.

Finance Companies

Finance companies are medium to short-term lenders to business. Some large finance companies are divisions of major banks (ESANDA and ANZ, AGC and Westpac,etc) They are funded by equity, investor deposits, preference share, and debentures. Finance companies are very active in the leasing business, particularly for motor vehicles and business equipment.

Superannuation funds

There are a large number of superannuation funds operating in Australia. Superannuation is a regular payment made into a fund by an employee or his employer toward a future pension. In Australia, a minimum proportion of income is required to be paid into a superannuation fund. The funds being held by these organisations has increased greatly in recent years.

The pool of funds available for business investment has grown to a significant level. AMP, MLC and Colonial First State have been traditional institutional investors in business. In recent times, Australians have taken advantage of Self managed Superannuation Funds (SMSF's). These are a growing source of funds for small business.

Life insurance companies

These companies sell policies to individuals to provide for their retirement. The accumulated funds are invested in properties, shares, and other financial assets, to earn income on behalf of policy holders. The larger companies are a significant source of investment funds for business. Life companies hold some of their long term investments in government backed activities such as infrastructure projects.

Unit trusts

Trusts are business entities which own assets on behalf of nominated beneficiaries and where profits may be distributed according to the rules of the trust. They are a relationship where a person (called the trustee) holds property or other assets on behalf of others.

Trusts may be managed by a company or financial institution and the trust may issue units to members which may be traded. Entities which are operated as trusts (with trustees and beneficiaries) include:
- Family Trusts where funds are set aside for the benefit of children or other family members- funds may be invested in any worthwhile project to earn income or grow capital funds
- SMSF's are trusts managing funds for retirement purposes- the funds may be invested in property, shares or other business assets. The income from these investments is taxed at a preferential rate, and accumulates for the benefit of the beneficiaries
- Unit Trusts are similar to family trusts,but may benefit unit holders who are not family members.

Australian Securities Exchange (ASX)

The Australian Securities Exchange (ASX) provides a forum for businesses and individuals to buy and sell shares. The following extract details the history and purpose of the Australian Securities Exchange:

The Australian Securities Exchange Limited (ASX) was formed in 1987 through the amalgamation of six independent stock exchanges that formerly operated in the state capital cities. Each of those exchanges had a history of share trading dating back to the last century.

ASX was originally a mutual organisation of stockbrokers, like its predecessor State stock exchanges. However, in 1996, its members decided to demutualise and list, which required legislation of the Australian parliament. The change of status took place on 13 October 1998, and the following day ASX listed on its market.

ASX operates Australia's primary national stock exchange for equities, derivatives and fixed interest securities and facilitates capital raisings for unlisted companies, using advanced computer systems for trading, settlement and issuer/investor matching that provide Australia-wide market access. It also provides comprehensive market data and information to a range of users. All these operations are underpinned by comprehensive information technology systems.

Ref: Australian Securities Exchange web site *www.asx.com.au*

Stock Exchange.

From the ASX website www.asx.com.au

ASX Group

ASX Group (ASX) is an umbrella brand developed to reflect the role of ASX Limited as the holding company of a group with a diverse range of market service activities linked by a common commitment to provide the infrastructure Australia needs to create a globally competitive capital market and a vibrant, robust economy.

ASX Group was created by the merger of the Australian Stock Exchange and the Sydney Futures Exchange in July 2006 and is today one of the world's top 10 listed exchange groups measured by market capitalisation.

ASX is a multi-asset class, vertically-integrated exchange group whose activities span primary and secondary market services, including the raising, allocation and hedging of capital flows, trading and price discovery (Australian Securities Exchange); central counterparty risk transfer (via subsidiaries of ASX Clearing Corporation); and securities settlement for both the equities and fixed income markets (via subsidiaries of ASX Settlement Corporation).

ASX functions as a market operator, clearing house and payments system facilitator. It also oversees compliance with its operating rules, promotes standards of corporate governance among Australia's listed companies and helps to educate retail investors.

The domestic and international customer base of ASX is diverse. It includes issuers (such as corporations and trusts) of a variety of listed securities and financial products; investment and trading banks; fund managers; hedge funds; commodity trading advisers; brokers and proprietary traders; market data vendors; and retail investors.

In addition to its role as a market operator, ASX relies on a range of subsidiary brands to monitor and enforce compliance with its operating rules. These subsidiaries are:

- Australian Securities Exchange - handles ASX's primary, secondary and derivative market services. It encompasses ASX (formerly Australian Stock Exchange) and ASX 24 (formerly Sydney Futures Exchange)
- ASX Clearing Corporation - is the brand under which ASX's clearing services are promoted. It encompasses ASX Clear (formerly the Australian Clearing House) and ASX Clear (Futures) (formerly SFE Clearing Corporation)
- ASX Settlement Corporation - is the brand under which ASX Group's settlement services are promoted. It encompasses ASX Settlement (formerly ASX Settlement and Transfer Corporation) and Austraclear
- ASX Compliance - is the brand under which services are provided to the ASX Group for the ongoing monitoring and enforcement of compliance with the ASX operating rules. This entity replaces ASX Markets Supervision.

The oversight work performed by ASX's subsidiaries ensures that it provides fair and reliable systems, processes and services that instill confidence in the markets that depend on its infrastructure.

Confidence in the operations of ASX is reinforced by the market supervision and regulatory role undertaken by the Australian Securities and Investments Commission (ASIC) across all trading venues and clearing and settlement facilities, as well as through the Reserve Bank of Australia's oversight of financial system stability. ASIC also supervises ASX's own compliance as a listed public company.

Influence of government

An important element of the Australian financial system is that it is an orderly one with many controls in place to ensure fair trading. Government impacts on business through a number of agencies:

- The Australian Securities and Investment Commission is the prime regulator of business and the financial system.
- The Australian Taxation Office (ATO) raises revenue from business and individuals.
- State authorities such as the Department of Fair Trading in NSW or Consumer Affairs in Victoria make regulations affecting business practices in those states.
- Occupational Health and Safety is regulated by a number of State, Federal and Local government agencies. Players in this area include Fire authorities, Health departments, Council advisers and inspectors, etc.
- Local government (through Local councils) influences hours of business and consumer and supplier access to places of business.
- The Fair Work Act 2009 (as amended 2010) has had a significant effect on relations between, business, the unions, and the workforce. (refer to the QANTAS dispute of 2011)

In 2011, the Federal Government's legislative program promises to have an increasing effect on business. The Federal Government has a number of proposed changes: Mining tax, Carbon tax, increases in compulsory superannuation; all these will bring fundamental changes to the business environment in the ensuing years.

Government is also an important consumer for Australian business and consumers have a significant impact on business.

ASIC

The Australian Securities and Investment Commission (ASIC) was set up in 1989 to administer corporations law in Australia. ASIC is a government body established by the Australian Securities and Investments Commission Act 1989 and began on 1 January 1 991 as the Australian Securities Commission, to administer the Corporations Law. It replaced the National Companies and Securities Commission (NCSC) and the Corporate Affairs offices of the States and Territories. In July 1998 it received new consumer protection responsibilities and its current name. The extract on the page opposite outlines the functions and powers vested in ASIC by the act.

Corporate Taxation

If a business makes a profit it will pay tax. The *company tax* rate is currently 30% on net profits. Taxation is used by governments to fund programs operated to benefit citizens. Large amounts of money are expended on infrastructure projects to enable the community to operate efficiently. Tax revenue is also used for welfare purposes: the government has a duty of care towards the less able.

Some businesses also pay State taxes, such as payroll tax. If a business is involved in trading, it will also pay GST (Goods and Services Tax) although GST is deductible where purchases are made for trading.

ASIC-What we do

ASIC is Australia's corporate, markets and financial services regulator.

We contribute to Australia's economic reputation and wellbeing by ensuring that Australia's financial markets are fair and transparent, supported by confident and informed investors and consumers.

We are an independent Commonwealth Government body. We are set up under and administer the Australian Securities and Investments Commission Act (ASIC Act), and we carry out most of our work under the Corporations Act.

The Australian Securities and Investments Commission Act 2001 requires us to:
- maintain, facilitate and improve the performance of the financial system and entities in it
- promote confident and informed participation by investors and consumers in the financial system
- administer the law effectively and with minimal procedural requirements
- enforce and give effect to the law
- receive, process and store, efficiently and quickly, information that is given to us
- make information about companies and other bodies available to the public as soon as practicable.

ASIC-Our powers

The laws we administer give us the facilitative, regulatory and enforcement powers necessary for us to perform our role. These include the power to:
- register companies and managed investment schemes
- grant Australian financial services licences and Australian credit licences
- register auditors and liquidators
- grant relief from various provisions of the legislation which we administer
- maintain publicly accessible registers of information about companies, financial services licensees and credit licensees
- make rules aimed at ensuring the integrity of financial markets
- stop the issue of financial products under defective disclosure documents
- investigate suspected breaches of the law and in so doing require people to produce books or answer questions at an examination
- issue infringement notices in relation to alleged breaches of some laws
- ban people from engaging in credit activities or providing financial services
- seek civil penalties from the courts
- commence prosecutions - these are generally conducted by the Commonwealth Director of Public Prosecutions, although there are some categories of matters which we prosecute ourselves.

ASIC has three full time Commissioners appointed by the Governor-General on the nomination of the Treasurer.

www.asic.gov.au

Global market influences

Business in Australia is increasingly influenced by global pressures. Changes in world commodity prices will have an effect on the Australian exports, particularly in Mining and Agriculture. We live in a global business environment and any movements in world economic activity will be reflected in the domestic economy. There have been two major crises in world economies in the last three years: the US recession led to the Global Financial Crisis (GFC), and in 2011 the debt crisis in the Eurozone (indicating possible loan defaults in Greece and Italy). Both these events in global markets have produced negative responses in Australia.

In early 2011, an International Monetary Fund (IMF) report suggested the world recovery since the GFC looked roughly like this:

- Recovery Proceeds in the United States
- A Gradual and Uneven Recovery Is under Way in Europe
- A Moderate Recovery Continues in the Commonwealth of Independent States
- Rapid Growth Continues in Asia
- Latin America Faces Buoyant External Conditions
- Growth Has Returned to Pre-crisis Rates in Many African Countries
- The Recovery in the Middle East and North Africa Region Faces an Uncertain Environment.

By November 2011, the IMF's policy towards global recovery had shifted. The president of the IMF in a speech to the 2011 International Finance Forum suggested that global recovery would depend on a number of factors.

- The success of the debt restructuring framework for the Eurozone agreed by finance ministers at the G20 meeting in October 2011, will be crucial to the survival of the Euro.
- Asia is propelling the global recovery, recovery will proceed if Asia continues to accept this role.
- Economic recovery needs to embrace the social needs of the population. There will be no lasting recovery without this.

This analysis serves to illustrate that global economic influences which were at one time predictable and long lasting, are now volatile, and of short term duration. The influences are both real and dynamic.

World economic recovery is delicate, and could easily stall. Possible triggers are:

- environmental disasters or terrorism
- countries defaulting on their loans.

The world recently suffered from a two-speed economic recovery where some sectors of the economy were doing well while other sectors were still feeling the effects of recession. In Australia, the minerals industry was booming due to export demand from China while the services sector continued to struggle.

Business Planning with a Global Perspective

Australian business managers must be mindful of these trends in Australian and world economic outlook when planning expansion either within Australia or globally. If the outlook is uncertain then expansion must be planned carefully. Otherwise bad investment choices may be made resulting in business losses.

This economic outlook can affect the availability of funds for business. Broadly, the availability of funds for investment and expansion depends on the level of domestic and overseas savings. Currently in Australia the savings pool is increasing, making the prospect for loans quite bright. International sources of funds are dependant on the strength of the global recovery.

The availability of funds for expansion is greatly influenced by interest rates. Overseas interest rates are traditionally low by Australian standards. Higher interest rates will attract foreign funds into Australia for investment purposes, increase the demand for Australian dollars and therefore push up its value. It will also have the effect of reducing demand for Australian exports because of the increased value of our dollar.

Likewise, low interest rates will divert foreign funds from Australia, reduce the demand for the Australian dollar and depreciate its value. This will have the effect of increasing demand for Australian exports because of the lower valued dollar.

Looked at from another perspective, Australian business people will tend to borrow overseas when domestic interest rates are high and borrow at home when domestic interest rates are low.

It is here that international finance markets come into play. The structure of these markets is complex and involves the interplay of banks, foreign exchange dealers, governments, businesses and even households around the world.

Businesses raise funds in order to grow and they will do this by either borrowing or by selling equity. When they deal overseas, rather than at home, they will deal with international credit markets to borrow funds or the offshore equities markets to raise funds by selling equity in the business. Either way they become exposed to the risks and advantages of changing exchange rates via the foreign exchange (forex) market. The forex market is where currencies are traded by financial institutions acting as buyers and sellers.

The international credit markets and offshore equities markets are also known as 'Euromarkets' which operate in Europe, North America and Asia. It is through Euromarkets that much overseas borrowing and investing takes place.

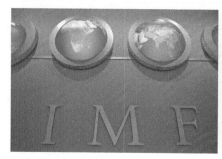

REVISION EXERCISES 3.2

1. What do you understand by the concepts of internal and external sources of finance?

   _____

   _____

   _____

2. What are retained profits?

   _____

   _____

   _____

3. What is meant by the term 'debt financing'?

   _____

   _____

   _____

4. What is an overdraft?

   _____

   _____

   _____

5. What is a commercial bill and what is it used for?

   _____

   _____

6. What is factoring?

   _____

   _____

   _____

7. What is a mortgage? And outline the two types of mortgage.

   _____

   _____

   _____

   _____

REVISION EXERCISES 3.2   **Page 2**

8. Define long-term borrowing.

_____

_____

_____

_____

9. What is a debenture?

_____

_____

_____

10. What are unsecured notes?

_____

_____

_____

11. Explain how leasing can be described as a form of finance.

_____

_____

_____

12. Define both 'equity' and 'owners equity'.

_____

_____

_____

_____

_____

13. List the four main advantages of using equity finance to grow a business. What is the main disadvantage?

1 _____

2 _____

3 _____

4 _____

REVISION EXERCISES 3.2 Page 3

14. Distinguish between 'new issues' and 'rights issues', 'share placements'
And 'share purchase plans'.

_____

_____

_____

15. Distinguish between banks, investment banks, finance companies,
superannuation funds and life insurance companies.

_____

_____

_____

_____

16. What is a 'Unit Trust'?

_____

_____

_____

17. What role does the ASX play in financial management?

_____

_____

_____

18. What is an investment bank?

_____

_____

_____

19. What role does the IMF play in financial management?

_____

_____

_____

_____

3.3 Processes of Financial Management

Planning and implementing

Once a business determines their sources of finance (debt or equity), they must plan their management strategies and take steps to convert these strategies into action.

Planning financial needs

Proper planning must start with an assessment of the present financial position. A business must have adequate cash flows so that it is able to pay any debts as they fall due. This assessment would consider:

- liquidity
- profitability
- efficiency
- rate of growth
- return on capital in the short, medium and long term.

Return on capital is typically expressed in terms of a ratio of net profit to Capital Invested. The usual name for this ratio is **Return on Investment** or **ROI**, calculated according to the formula below:

$$\text{Return on Investment} = \frac{\text{Net Profit}}{\text{Capital}} \times \frac{100}{1} \%$$

When a business purchases capital equipment to be used in operations, the owners expect a return on that investment. For example, the expenditure on a new computerised manufacturing plant is usually undertaken in the light of the anticipated increased returns it will bring to the business.

There are always competing objectives in this situation. The purchase of new capital equipment might reduce the liquidity of the business for a period of time. However, there is always the objective of increased profitability and growth that might counter the short term problem with liquidity.

Central to all of this is the necessity to remain solvent. This, in its simplest terms, is the requirement that the business does not run out of cash. An insolvent business will cease to operate and will be wound up. Any investment decisions must be undertaken without using up the working funds needed to meet ongoing commitments.

When acquiring additional finance it is appropriate to investigate :

- **Sources of finance:**
  - bank finance is relatively inexpensive if the business has security.
  - credit unions will provide funds for approved purposes.
  - merchant banks will provide funds as venture capital or asset buyouts.
  - building societies will provide funds for property purchases or for personal loans.
  - finance companies will assist with working capital or equipment finance.
  - financial markets will provide funds for business from the sale of shares or the issuing of debentures.
  - family & friends.. the lender of last resort.
- **Types of finance** (debt or equity). A careful manager will balance these alternate sources in the interest of all stakeholders.
- **Amount of finance required.** This a matter of judgment, to be determined in the light of finance costs, profitability, cash flow needs, return on investment, and dividend expectations.
- **Repayment period.** This is determined by cash flow considerations.
- **Repayment method.** This is determined by the source and type of funds:
  - Debt finance will eventually need to be repaid
  - If equity finance is used, the capital will remain with the business as shareholders funds, but there will be an annual cost as dividends will usually be paid to shareholders.
- **Uses of the finance:**
  - Funds may used to improve the **liquidity** of the business, reducing operating costs.
  - Financing new product development may result in improved **profitability.**
  - Purchase new capital equipment or new accounting systems will improve **efficiency.**
  - Finance for a new project may result in business **growth** by opening new markets.
  - Purchase of new technology may improve **return on capital**.

Developing Budgets

Budgets are projections of future operating results based on planning. The business predicts how, when and why its future expenditure will be incurred. It will also estimate how, when and from what direction its receipts will come. Part of this process is predicting the impact of external factors. A sophisticated budget will analyse possible outcomes and develop contingency plans based on different predictions of future events.

- Financial planners will develop weekly, monthly, yearly, five-yearly, and longer term budgets.
- Budgeting is an interactive process.
  - Financial management will involve continual comparison of actual results with those predicted in the budget.
  - Budgets will be continuously revised in the light of new information and events.
  - New investment decisions will need to be made as plans and strategies are modified.
  - New budgets will need to take these new plans into account.

Maintaining record systems

Good record keeping systems are essential to enable the manager to stay in touch with what is happening within the business. Accurate and timely accounting reports provided to management will monitor:

- sales performance
- cash flow (This includes expenditure and collection of accounts receivable)
- liquidity and Solvency
- productivity and efficiency.

If the expected result is not being achieved then good records will enable the manager to take corrective action. This could relate to a liquidity, solvency or efficiency problem. If the business is moving along as expected financially, appropriate records systems provide the manager with a source of information to monitor the progress of the business.

Increasingly, a business will rely on records generated electronically. Even very small businesses have access to accounting software that will generate and store records. Larger businesses have efficient Management Information Systems (MIS) which can store large amounts of vital financial information from various departments and make it available to those who require it in the business.

Minimising financial risk and losses

Financial risk might arise from a number of sources. A bad investment decision may increase the likely hood of financial loss. A marketing program may collapse reducing revenue. An overseas expansion program may not meet expectations, requiring increased funds for a longer than expected term. The investment funds may be put at risk, or lost completely. Investment advice from external sources may be unreliable, or not take unexpected factors into account. Significant sources of risk include:

- Bad debts may reduce profitability. Procedures need to be put in place to ensure that debts are collected on time and that 'bad debts' are minimised.
- Liquidity and Solvency : a highly geared business will be at risk if economic conditions vary unexpectedly. Advice should be obtained from the business accountant or bank, and in any case the manager should have contingency plans in place when developing budgets.
- Cash flow, profitability and turnover must be monitored together. A business needs to be profitable to satisfy shareholder's dividend expectations. A steady or increasing turnover is an indication that the business is meeting its market expectations. A sound cash flow ensures the business remains viable, collects its revenue and pays its bills.

Businesses that trade globally have other financial risks including:

- **Exchange rate risks.** This refers to the risk of losing money on international transactions as a result of changes in the exchange rate. Depreciation of the Australian dollar or an appreciation of the overseas currency forces the Australian business to take a loss on the transaction. This can be protected against by hedging against the risk of currency fluctuations. The price paid for a future transaction is fixed at current rates.
- **Political and default risk.** This risk is associated with political and economic uncertainty in the overseas country. The GFC and Euro Zone crises of 2008 and 2011 are real-life examples of this.
- **Asset Insurance and Liability Insurance**. Business must ensure that there is an adequate level in insurance on their plant and buildings in addition to public liability and professional liability insurance etc.

Financial controls

Controlling is the setting of standards, measuring performance and taking corrective action if necessary. Financial controls include budgets, the various financial statements and the use of financial ratios. These three controls will guide the manager towards the correct decisions regarding:

- liquidity
- profitability
- efficiency
- future growth of the business.

They can measure the actual financial performance of the business against planned performance and take corrective action if necessary.

Debt and equity financing

A business may use debt finance, equity finance, or a combination of both. Appropriate debt to equity ratios are influenced by the type of industry and level of cash flow. For example, a business with quick revenue stream following an outflow of funds may use only equity finance. (e.g. a greengrocer may buy his produce from the markets using cash, and sell through his store recouping his money within a week.)

A grower, on the other hand, may obtain bank finance for the growing season, needing to incur expenses at the time of planting, and recouping his funds after harvesting. A rich farmer might fund his business from equity, or a combination of debt and equity.

Debt Finance

A business adopting debt finance may match the type of finance to the purpose required. For example, overdrafts are suitable for short-term loan purposes and mortgages are usual for long-term loan purposes. A business with a sound cash flow will have an ability to take on higher levels of debt.

The advantages of debt include:

- flexible repayment periods available
- there is no initial expensive outlay
- interest on repayments is tax deductible
- ownership and control of the business remains with the owners.

The disadvantages of debt include:

- over the life of the loan, interest rates may rise, increasing repayments
- increased gearing introduces increased financial risk to the business
- the loan must be repaid in full.

Equity Finance

A business adopting equity finance will obtain funds without the burden of increased liabilities. Payments for this additional finance need only to be made if the business makes a profit. This has a positive effect on the cash flow.

The advantages of using equity finance are:
- there is no repayment required
- no interest charges
- the return on the funds is determined by business performance and does not add to gearing or risk to the business.

The disadvantage of using equity finance is:
- selling shares is selling part of the business
- shareholders have a claim on the business profits
- dividends paid to shareholders are not tax deductible.

Matching the terms and source of finance to business needs

The source of finance that each business will use depends on the type of business involved. A business needs to match the source of funds to its needs and structure. Most businesses will use a combination of internal and external sources of finance. They are likely to access both debt and equity finance. It is important to note that there is no correct source of finance that a business must use but the following will provide a useful guideline.

A small business is likely to use:
- internal sources may be retained profits or money from personal savings.
- external sources may be bank overdraft or property mortgage.

A larger business is likely to use:
- internal sources in the form of retained profits and
- external sources could be bank bills or debentures
- other sources of finance such as leasing, factoring, venture capital and grants.

The purpose of the loan will also influence the type of finance provided. An overdraft is ideal to cover short term debts or when extra working capital is needed. If funds are required for longer periods, the business may seek mortgage funds, Other sources of funds may be appropriate for a larger business that wants to retain a reasonable level of working capital. In this case leasing and factoring would be appropriate. The business looking to expand into new territories may seek venture capital or government grants. Such funds may come from long-term bank borrowings, or, in the case of venture capital, from private equity funds provided by a merchant bank.

The process of planning for and maintaining the most appropriate financial mix for the business is one of the most critical management functions. Ideas vary and there can be no 100% equation for every business. As any business grows it will develop a financial strategy. Capital will be needed to replace worn out or obsolete equipment, to buy new premises or establish new locations. Managers of growing businesses will always have to decide whether investments in new assets should be financed by debt or equity.

Regardless of which form of finance is used, there are always some risks associated. With debt finance, the main risk is being able to repay the loan from the profits of the business. If the business is not profitable, then the business will not be able to repay. Secondly, if interest rates increase greatly, the business might also find itself in trouble due to the business being too highly geared.

Gearing/leverage refers to the ratio of debt to equity that a business has. The higher the level of borrowing a business has compared to its equity, then the more highly geared it is said to be. Gearing or borrowing is generally a good thing for a business because it allows that business to expand or purchase new plant and equipment. The problem arises if the business is too highly geared. However, the level of gearing that is suitable for a particular business depends on the particular business. For example, a business that doesn't have a regular cash flow or one that is experiencing profitability difficulties would be unwise to gear too highly.

If trading conditions decline or interest rates rise, the business may find itself unable to repay its loans. If this occurs it causes liquidity problems and eventually insolvency.

Monitoring and controlling

It is important to monitor and control the flow of funds into and out of a business so that the manager can plan their financial activities. To monitor and control the manager uses:
- cash flow statements
- income statements
- balance sheets.

Cash flow statements

A cash flow statement is a device used by a business manager to monitor the flow of funds. It is a summary of the movements of cash over a given period of time. It provides managers with useful information for making up a budget for the next year. It shows the manager at a glance, the receipts and payments the business has made for that month.

In its simplest form it looks at:

Opening balance for the month + cash in - cash out= closing balance

The cash flow statement is often regarded as a planning tool because the business manager can use the information contained in it to plan future expenditure. For example, it tells the manager how much cash comes in each month and which month is the busiest and which month is quietest. It tells the manager how much has been spent on the various expenses such as wages, insurance, advertising, office expenses, telephone and rent etc.

Once these figures have been calculated, the manager can make decisions regarding ways of paying some of these expenses. For example:

- Insurance can be a large expense that may come at a quiet time of the year, so it may be decided to pay the insurance bills by the month in order to spread the load.
- Information for making a budget for next year can be determined.
- It includes payments made for assets or loan repayments.
- The cash flow statement allows investors to understand how a company's operations are running, where its money is coming from, and how it is being spent.

A cash flow statement is fairly simple to construct. The opening balance at the beginning of each month is carried across from the closing balance of the previous month. All of the expenses are added up and then subtracted from the income of that month leaving a closing balance which is then transferred across as the opening balance for the next month and so on. It must be noted that some businesses will have some months where they have a negative cash flow. This may happen say if the businesses closes down over Christmas or if the business has certain months of the year where custom is very slow. This is not a major problem if there are other months where a positive cash flow is sufficient to cover the slow months. A typical cash flow statement for a small business can be seen below.

	J	A	S	O	N	D	J	F	M	A	M	J
B/F	0	4,255	10,766	15,796	23,696	27,286	26,016	24,281	25,361	24,676	30,501	36,716
Rent	500	500	500	500	500	500	500	500	500	500	500	500
Internet/web	30	30	30	30	30	30	30	30	30	30	30	30
Advertising	585	790	600	450	100	50	500	500	650	450	150	250
Phone/fax	45	50	35	40	50	20	10	70	35	40	40	
Wages	925	934	845	790	480	300	500	900	900	780	770	900
Bank expenses	35	25	20	25	45	55	45	20	40	45	25	30

The Income/Revenue/Profit & Loss/ Statement

This statement provides a summary of the trading operations of a business for a given period of time (usually one month or a year). This statement has two parts. The first part shows the total of the sales minus the costs of making those sales (known as the cost of goods sold). This gives us gross profit. Subtracted from this figure are all administrative costs required to run the business such as rent, advertising cleaning and telephone. This then gives net profit. This statement contains two items or categories—income and expenditure. Therefore, the Income Statement equation is I-E = P or Income minus Expenditure equals Profit. It should also be noted that the income statement is also known as a Revenue or Profit & Loss Statement

At this point it is important to examine each of the components of the income statement.

Revenue

Revenue is the income received from the sale of the goods and/or services of the business. There are two basic ways of measuring revenue:

1. by measuring the cost of the sales at the time of payment and the cash is received or
2. if the goods are sold on credit, it can be measured by the promise by the customer to pay in the future (an account receivable).

Expenses

Expenses are the cost of the goods and services used in earning the revenue over the period. As with revenue there are two basic ways of measuring expenses:

1. by measuring the amount at the time of incurring the expense and when the expense is paid for or
2. if the goods are purchased on credit, it can be measured by the promise to pay the supplier in the future (an account payable).

In its simplest form an income statement an income statement looks like the example below.

Income Statement: Watt and Associates for the month ended June 2013

Sales		700,000
Less Cost of Goods Sold		
Opening stock	40,000	
Plus purchases	300,000	
	340,000	
Less closing stock	60,000	
	280,000	280,000
Gross profit		420,000
Less admin expenses		
Advertising	40,000	
Rent	60,000	
General expenses	120,000	
	220,000	220,000
Net profit		200,000

The Balance Sheet

This statement gives a summary of a businesses' financial position as at a particular point in time. It shows the assets and liabilities of the business together with the value of owners equity in the business.

The assets consist of current assets and non-current assets. Current assets consist of assets that can be turned into cash in a short period of time (usually within the accounting period). Current assets include cash, accounts receivable, inventories (which can be turned to cash quickly) and cash paid in advance. Non-current assets are those assets that are held for a longer period of time (longer than the accounting period) and may be up to several years because of the nature of those assets. Non-current assets include:

■ fixed assets such as motor vehicles, plant & equipment and buildings
■ investments which include shares in other companies
■ intangibles such as trademarks, goodwill and patents.

Liabilities also consist of current liabilities and non-current liabilities. Current liabilities are liabilities that may be called on in the short term (within one accounting period) and include accounts payable and overdrafts. Non-current liabilities are held for a longer period of time (usually several years) and include mortgages and long-term borrowings.

Owners equity are the assets that the business holds on behalf of the owners and includes shares and retained profits. The retained profits may be used by the business for expansion purposes or drawn out of the business for the owners to use or pay as dividends to shareholders. We can see below an example of a balance sheet.

Balance Sheet of Watt and Associates: As at 30 June 2013

ASSETS			LIABILITIES		
Current Assets			**Current Liabilities**		
Cash	50,000		Accts payable	100,000	
Accts receivable	70,000		Overdraft	10,000	
Inventory	60,000				110,000
		180,000			
Non Current Assets			**Non Current Liabilities**		
Land & Buildings	900,000		Mortgage	500,000	
Office fittings	400,000				500,000
		1,300,000			
			Owners Equity		
			Capital	670,000	
			Net Profit	200,000	
					870,000
		1,480,000			1,480,000

The Accounting equation and relationships

The accounting equation refers to the relationship between the businesses assets (what it owns) and its liabilities and owners equity (what it owes). The liabilities are owed to external parties such as creditors (long and short term). Owners equity is what the business owes its owners/shareholders. The accounting equation is expressed in the following way:

Assets = liabilities + Owners equity

Analysing Financial Information

Business managers need to understand financial reports to make good business decisions.

The raw figures themselves have little meaning as far as the performance of the business is concerned.

Managers use a number of devices, usually in the form of financial ratios to interpret results in a meaningful way.

Ratios are used to analyse:
- liquidity
- gearing
- profitability
- efficiency

Liquidity

Liquidity refers to the ability of a business to pay its short term debts when they fall due. In order to tell if the business is able to do this, the following ratios can be applied using the balance sheet.

$$\text{Current Ratio} = \frac{\text{Current Assets}}{\text{Current Liabilities}}$$

$$= \frac{\$180,000}{\$110,000}$$

$$= 1.63:1$$

In this case Watt and Associates have $1.63 in Current assets for every $1 in current liabilities. Traditionally a figure of 2:1 was regarded as an acceptable figure, however now with improved inventory management such as JIT, a lower figure is now considered acceptable. It should also be noted that this acceptable figure would also depend on the industry. Such an industry would be one where there was a high level of cash flow. Indeed some industries can work satisfactorily with a ratio of 1:1.

Gearing

Debt to equity (Solvency) refers to the ability of a business to meet its long term commitments such as a mortgage.

$$\text{Debt to Equity Ratio} = \frac{\text{Total Liabilities}}{\text{Total Equity}}$$

$$= \frac{\$610,000}{\$870,000}$$

$$= 0.7:1$$

This ratio provides a measure of the extent to which the business relies on borrowed funds to finance its operations. The higher the debt/equity ratio, the greater the reliance on borrowed funds. A business that relies too heavily on borrowed funds is said to be highly geared.

In this case for every 70c of liabilities there is $1 of equity which means that the business is able to meet its long term debts.

As a general rule, a debt to equity ratio of less than 100% is considered to be acceptable although this ratio can vary widely between industries. Excessive gearing levels have contributed to many corporate collapses in recent years. However, it should be noted that if gearing is too low, then management may be losing profitable investment opportunities. It could indicate a failure on the part of management to effectively utilise debt. The challenge for management is to select an appropriate gearing level. A company is most effective when it has a mixture of debt and equity.

Profitability

Profitability is a measure of how well a business is using the funds provided by its owners to return a good profit. This is a good indicator of its financial well-being of the business and as a measure of how well it is being managed, Poor earnings can have a detrimental effect on the company's share price and its ability to pay dividends to share holders.

The following ratios can be used to assess the profitability of Watt and Associates.

$$\text{Gross profit Ratio} = \frac{\text{Gross profit}}{\text{sales}} \times \frac{100}{1}\%$$

$$= \frac{\$420,000}{\$700,000} \times \frac{100}{1}\%$$

$$= 60\%$$

There is no hard and fast rule as to what is a good profit level except to say that the higher the better. The actual figure may be good or bad depending on the industry and the sector of the industry that the business is in. For example, Woolworths would have a much lower gross profit than a corner store. For Watt and Associates a gross profit of 60% means that each dollar of sales it is producing 60c of gross profit.

$$\text{Net profit Ratio} = \frac{\text{Net Profit}}{\text{sales}} \times \frac{100}{1}\%$$

$$= \frac{\$200,000}{\$700,000} \times \frac{100}{1}\%$$

$$= 28.5\%$$

The net profit margin measures the level of profit after operating costs and other expenses have been deducted from the gross profit. In the case of Watt and Associates, the business is generating 28.5% net profit from the sales made.

With both figures, they should be compared to either the industry average or past performance.

The final ratio to be considered is Return on Owners Equity. This ratio measures the net profit that is obtained as a return on owners invested funds. As with all profitability ratios, the higher the figure the better but also it gives potential investors an insight into the profitability of the business from an investment point of view.

$$\text{Return on Equity} = \frac{\text{Net Profit}}{\text{Total equity}} \times \frac{100}{1}$$

$$= \frac{\$200,000}{\$870,000} \times \frac{100}{1}\%$$

$$= 23\%$$

Here Watt and Associates must look for trends from one year to the next, compare their performance with other businesses and consider alternative investments in new products or diversify their interests if results are not satisfactory. In this case it would seem that Watt and Associates are achieving a most satisfactory level of profitability on funds invested.

Efficiency

Efficiency relates to how well something is being done and efficiency ratios provide the means of measuring that efficiency. The two ratios we will consider here are the expense ratio and the accounts receivable turnover ratio.

Expenses are very important to a business because many a business has failed because it has failed to monitor its expenses. This ratio is particularly useful if it is compared against industry averages or the past performance of the business.

The Expense ratio relates sales figures to the expenses incurred in making those sales. For Watt & Associates, the following Expense ratio would apply:

$$\text{Expense Ratio} = \frac{\text{Total Expenses}}{\text{sales}} \times \frac{100}{1}$$

$$= \frac{\$220,000}{\$700,000} \times \frac{100}{1}\%$$

$$= 31.5\%$$

This means that for every $1 of sales 31.5c s taken up in operating expenses.

Expenses can be further divided up into selling, financial and general expenses on the Profit & Loss statement.

The Accounts Receivable Turnover ratio measures how efficiently the business is collecting its debts i.e. how efficient the credit policy of the business is. In the case of Watt & Associates the following would apply.

$$\text{Accounts receivable Turnover} = \frac{\text{Sales}}{\text{Accounts Receivable}}$$

$$= \frac{\$700,000}{\$70,000}$$

$$= 10$$

In this case Watt & Associates has an annual revenue equal to 10 times the level of accounts receivable. This equates their customers taking on average 36.5 days to pay for credit sales. Most businesses work on credit terms of 30, 60 or in some cases 90 days. Depending on the credit policy of Watt & Associates, a judgment can be made regarding the efficiency of their credit policy.

Comparative ratio analysis

Ratios are used mainly for comparison purposes and to give meaning to raw figures. Business may use ratios for comparisons to analyse:
- trends over time
- analysis of similar types of businesses in similar industries
- comparisons with industry averages.

With each of the ratios the business manager will determine if a trend is a good one or a bad one. For example, if the gross profit ratio of a business has declined over a period of time then management would need to look at the two possible causes e.g. cost of goods sold or sales and decide what to do.

When comparing similar businesses/industries, the manager will consider what is an appropriate ratio for the business or industry. For a supermarket, the net profit ratio may be much lower than a corner store. The supermarket with larger turnover (volume of sales) will operate with a smaller profit margin per item.

Expense ratios of businesses in the same industry can be compared to see if they are in line with their competitors. If not, corrective action can be taken. When measuring against common standards, we mean that the manager is measuring against what is regarded as an acceptable benchmark.

Government agencies such as the ATO have data on businesses in many industries. They develop industry averages of accounting ratios, especially net profit ratio (NPR) and Return on Investment(ROI). This data is used when assessing taxation returns submitted by business. Financial managers should periodically compare their calculated ratios with the industry averages to keep track of the way the business is performing.

Limitations of financial reports

Financial reports are essential documents but have their limitations. They are only as accurate as the assumptions on which they are based, as the following shows:

- Adjusted for normalised earnings which are earnings adjusted for cyclical ups and downs in the economy. On the balance sheet, earnings are adjusted to remove unusual or one-time influences.
- Capitalising expenses involves the tendency to hide reasonable operating costs, such as maintenance, by physically changing the way the asset is managed.
- Debt repayments can be moved from one accounting period to another to help with taxation regulations.
- Sometimes the notes to the financial statements can be misleading or confusing.
- Businesses may use different report formats and ratios that may confuse or mislead those reading them. This may make their interpretation and comparisons over time difficult.
- The use of 'historic cost' can constitute a major limitation. Historic cost is the practice of valuing assets at the time of purchase. In the mean time those assets such as land and buildings may have appreciated greatly. On the other hand, assets such as equipment (particularly computer equipment) may have depreciated. In this way valuations may be distorted and not reflect the real situation.
- The business may have diversified into other product areas or been taken over by a competitor. This may make it difficult to compare business results over time and with industry benchmarks.
- Annual reports for the end of the financial year are often not published until months afterwards making them out of date and in many cases irrelevant.
- Businesses often only provide the absolute minimum accounting information necessary. This then doesn't show a true picture of the business.
- Items such as goodwill (the reputation of the business) and other intangibles such as patents, copyrights, trademarks and brand names are often difficult to quantify.
- Occasionally businesses may publish its financial reports using 'creative accounting' giving the wrong impression due to the incorrect asset value of equipment.

Ethical issues related to financial reports

Ethics are very important in business, because without ethics there can be no trust. This is particularly true in the case of finance and management. Audited accounts, inappropriate cut off periods and misuse of funds are some of the important aspects of ethical issues related to financial reports.

Audited accounts

It is a universal and legal practice for the accounts of public companies to be audited by a team of independent accountants (auditors) to test for authenticity, truth and fairness, in particular the misuse of funds. All stakeholders such as investors and customers need to be confident that the businesses' accounts are as they should be.

While there is a legal requirement for public companies to have their accounts audited, other businesses and even sporting organisations also have their accounts audited for the sake of ethics and transparency.

Inappropriate cut off periods

Cut off periods for reports must be appropriate. By this we mean that the report should represent a period of time when income and expenditure for that time period are included in the same report. Using a simplistic example, if a business had an income of $5 million for a given three month period and towards that time, there were expenses of $6 million then they should be included in the same report. However the finance manager might decide to bring the cut-off period just before the $6 million has to be paid out and so the report will be misleading and inappropriate.

Misuse of funds

Regular checks must be made by auditors and other qualified internal personnel to ensure that there is no misuse of funds. The business must develop an effective internal control system for this procedure. It is not only funds that can be misappropriated in a business but also inventory. Penalties need to be well known to staff to help prevent misuse of funds.

Corporate raiders and asset stripping

Corporate raiding involves a business buying a large number of shares in another company with the aim of gaining control of that company. Usually the assets and share value of the company being raided is low because of poor management and performance or because the assets are valued at low historically undervalued levels. The raid would force up the value of the shares. The raider could then sell the shares purchased at a substantial profit.

Asset stripping, involves a company purchasing a controlling interest in another (usually poorly performing) company and then disposing of (stripping) the under-valued assets for a quick profit at a slightly higher price.

In cases where a business is about to close down, the directors may restructure the company by forming a number of separate companies controlled by a single holding company. The holding company could then strip the assets of the smaller companies, leaving employees without their entitlements such as holiday, long-service leave and superannuation entitlements.

REVISION QUESTIONS 3.3

1. Explain why it is important for a business to plan its financial needs.

   _____

   _____

   _____

2. What is meant by the term 'return on capital'?

   _____

   _____

   _____

3. What is the importance of budgets to business?

   _____

   _____

   _____

4. What is the importance of maintaining record systems?

   _____

   _____

   _____

5. Outline the **four** broad ways in which businesses can minimise financial risks and losses.

   _____

   _____

   _____

   _____

6. What are financial controls and what do they include?

   _____

   _____

   _____

7. Explain the difference between debt and equity finance.

_____

_____

_____

_____

_____

_____

_____

8. Outline the **four** advantages of debt finance and the two disadvantages of debt finance.

_____

_____

_____

_____

9. Outline the **four** advantages of equity finance and the three disadvantages of equity finance.

_____

_____

_____

_____

10. Outline the ways business matches the terms and sources of finance to match their business needs.

_____

_____

_____

_____

_____

_____

_____

REVISION QUESTIONS 3.3

11. What is a 'cash flow statement'?

_____

_____

_____

_____

12. What is an 'Income statement'?

_____

_____

_____

_____

What else is the income statement known as?

_____

_____

_____

_____

13. Describe what a 'balance sheet' is and describe its components.

_____

_____

_____

_____

_____

_____

14. Write out the accounting equation.

_____

_____

_____

_____

_____

REVISION QUESTIONS 3.3 Page 4

15. Define liquidity, gearing, profitability and efficiency and write out the ratios for each.

_____

_____

_____

_____

_____

16. What are the three areas of comparison that accountants use with ratios?

_____

_____

_____

_____

_____

17. List **six** limitations of financial reports

_____

_____

_____

_____

_____

_____

18. Describe **three** ethical issues that have to be considered with financial reports.

_____

_____

_____

_____

_____

_____

3.4 Financial Management Strategies

Cash flow management

Cash flow statements have been discussed earlier in this topic and it is worth repeating that information here.

A cash flow statement is a summary of the movements of cash during a given period of time. It also provides managers with useful information for making up a budget for the next year. It shows the manager at a glance, the receipts and payments the business has made for that month.

Complementing the *balance sheet* and *income statement*, the *cash flow* statement records the amounts of *cash* entering and leaving a business usually on a monthly basis. It helps managers identify the receipts and payments of the business and the current cash position at the end of each month. In its simplest form it looks at:

Opening balance for the month + cash in - cash out = closing balance

The cash flow statement is often regarded as a planning tool because the business manager can use the information contained in it to plan future expenditure. For example, it tells the manager how much cash comes in each month and which month is the busiest and which month is quietest. It tells the manager how much has been spent on the various expenses such as wages, insurance, advertising, office expenses, telephone and rent etc.

Once these figures have been calculated, the manager can make decisions regarding ways of paying some of these expenses. For example insurance can be a large expense that may come at a quiet time of the year, so it may be decided to pay the insurance bills by the month in order to spread the load. It also provides useful information for making a budget for next year. It includes payments made for assets or loan repayments. The cash flow statement allows investors to understand how a company's operations are running, where its money is coming from, and how it is being spent.

However it is in this section that we look at how we manage our finances via the cash flow statement. Cash flow is the most important aspect of success because without sufficient cash flow a business will fail in a short period of time. There are several ways in which cash flow statements can help a business. There are several aspects cash flow statements that we will look at and they are distribution of payments, discounts for early payments and factoring.

Distribution of payments

Earning revenue from sales is one part of the equation, the other part is making payments to creditors. Planning for expenditure is very important because business expenditure, like income, usually doesn't come such that it is spread evenly across the year at the convenience of the business manager.

The most common example is that of a wool or wheat farmer who may receive a cheque for their produce only a couple of times a year. They need to make those funds last until the next cheque and therefore budget to make payments for farm (business) expenses during that period without overspending and finding themselves short of cash (liquidity) before the next cheque arrives. The same goes for those rural producers who may have bad seasons due to drought, flood or poor economic conditions. These conditions may even last for several years. In each case careful cash flow management is required.

Businesses in other industries may need to spread their payments across a year to avoid such things as fixed expenses such as insurance, vehicle registrations and council rates, failing at a time when business is quiet. This is particularly for the small business that is less able to bare a large number of expenses all at once.

There are several strategies that can be put in place such as:
- arranging to pay these bills monthly
- using trade credit in order to pay part of the debt when the business has a higher level of income
- paying bills at the latest possible time taking advantage of the interest savings by holding on to money as long as possible. Over a period of a year the savings could be considerable.
- using credit cards to pay bills. The repayments can be spread over a period of time.
- renegotiating repayments if difficulties are being experienced. Creditors will nearly always cooperate because they would prefer later or smaller payments to not receiving their money at all i.e. incurring a bad debt.

Discounts for early payments

Many businesses offer discounts to debtors for early payments as a means of improving cash flow. The industry norm for payments is 30 days. However many businesses offer a discount if the bill is paid early. This discount encourages debtors to pay during this time period because the discount may be a substantial sum of money and therefore saving.

Factoring

This is the selling of accounts receivable to a financier. This is regarded as an important source of finance because the business is receiving immediate funds to use as working capital. It works this way. A business sells its accounts receivable to a factoring company at a discount rate.

The factoring company then collects those accounts receivable. The difference between the figure that the accounts receivable were for and what they are collected for is the profit taken by the factoring company. For example, if a business has $100,000 worth of accounts receivable that are difficult to collect, it may sell those accounts for say $95,000. Even though the business doesn't get all of its money, it receives most of it immediately. Sometimes the business doesn't receive it at all. The firm can now continue on with its business. In the mean time the factoring company collects the accounts receivable taking $5,000 profit.

Working capital management

Working capital is the funds invested in short-term assets such as cash, short-term securities, accounts receivable and inventories less short-term liabilities. i.e. Current assets minus Current liabilities.

One can see these items on a typical balance sheet with the short-term assets such as cash, short-term securities, accounts receivable and inventories under Current assets and under Current liabilities we have short-term liabilities such as accounts payable or overdraft. These funds are very liquid i.e. can be converted into cash very quickly for the purposes of paying short-term debts as they fall due.

The working capital ratio is simply the ratio of current assets to current liabilities. N.B. This has been referred to under ratios as the liquidity ratio or the current ratio. As we have seen it is expressed as:

Current assets ÷ current liabilites = working capital

Current liabilities

Using the balance sheet below if the balance sheet of that business showed that its current assets totalled $24,000 and its current liabilities totalled $6,000 then it would have a working capital ratio of 4:1.

In other words for every $4 worth of current assets it has $1 worth of current liabilities. In this case the business is very secure in terms of being able to pay its short-term debts/bills. It has a positive working capital. This ratio is also known as the current ratio.

BALANCE SHEET OF HANNAH/MATTHEW & ASSOCIATES					
Assets			**Liabilities**		
Current			Current		
Cash	4,000		Accounts payable	1,000	
Short Term Securities	8,000		Overdraft	5,000	6,000
Accounts Receivable	2,000				
Inventories	10,000	24,000	Non Current		
Non Current			Mortgage	50,000	50,000
Plant & Machinery	100,000	100,000			
			Owners Equity		
			Capital	43,000	
			Net Profit	25,000	68,000
		$124,000			**$124,000**

The management of working capital is important to the day-to-day running of a business because any business must be able to pay debts as they fall due.

The other aspect of efficient working capital management relates very much to the ratio above. While the figure of 4:1 would seem very comfortable in terms of being able to pay short-term debts/bills, the business needs to monitor the figure and not allow the ratio to become too large because some of the surplus liquidity could be used for other, more profitable purposes such as investing in new plant and equipment or increased marketing.

The important factor here is the industry in which the business is operating. If the business is in an industry which has a predictable and constant cash flow, then the current ratio not be as high as a business that doesn't have this predictable and constant cash flow.

Control of current assets- cash, receivables, inventories

This is money from cash and credit sales that a business receives. The controlling of cash and receivables is a delicate balance and requires a budget which outlines the anticipated cash inflows and outflows over a period of time.

In terms of cash for example, a fruit juice distributing business will have its peak times where the inflow of cash is likely to be at its greatest during the warmer months of Summer. During Winter when sales drop off, the operator of the business would need to ensure that he/she has sufficient cash to meet the regular fixed expenses such as registration, insurance or repayments on their delivery vehicle. In this case the manager would need to try to spread the costs across the year by say, paying the vehicle insurance by the month or by budgeting to have funds to pay the vehicle registration when it falls due.

Leasing can also be used as a method of maintaining cash/working capital by preventing expensive outlays on expensive equipment. An added benefit is the fact that the costs of leasing are easier to quantify than depreciation. Leasing preserves working capital in the short-term.

Receivables can be costly if debts are not repaid. Trade credit is often extended to valuable customers. As a way of managing their receivables , a business must consider the limit to which it will issue that credit i.e. a credit limit. As a further means of managing their receivables they must also consider provisions for early payment (such as discounts---discussed earlier), credit period (extended and ongoing credit may be granted to valuable customers) and the credit rating of the customer being dealt with. In this way a stringent credit policy must be developed and adhered to if the business is to be sure of collecting most if not all of their receivables. Many businesses often factor their debts in order to get their receivables as quickly as possible.

Because credit can be costly if debts are not repaid it is important that a stringent credit policy be developed and adhered to if the business is to be sure of collecting most if not all of their receivables. Many businesses often factor their debts in order to get their receivables as quickly as possible. As discussed above, a factor is a financial institution that purchases the accounts receivable of a business and then collect them from those who owe the debt. The seller of the debt gets the money straight away less a certain percentage, but at least they don't have to spend the time chasing up potentially bad debts.

Inventories consist of raw materials, goods in transit and complete and incomplete work (work in progress). Inventories are expensive and can often comprise 50% of working capital. They are a major source of revenue and for this reason must be efficiently managed.

It can be expensive to carry too much inventory. There are storage costs as well as the costs of having large amounts of cash tied up sitting on shelves (especially if it is not selling).

The most efficient method of inventory management is the Just-in-Time (JIT) inventory management. JIT inventory management is the holding of a minimum quantity of stock necessary to run a business and therefore keep costs to a minimum and liquidity to a maximum.

However the level of inventories held by a business will also depend on:
- the levels of stock required to run the business
- the reliability and frequency of deliveries
- the type of product. If a product is perishable then only small stocks will be held. The same holds true if the product is a seasonal one such as a fashion item.
- insurance and security considerations. Inventory that is expensive to insure or has the potential for theft will be kept in smaller quantities
- the efficiency of the control process i.e. the responsiveness of the business in ordering and acquiring new stock.

Control of current liabilities- payables, loans, overdrafts

Current liabilities are debts that must be paid within the current accounting period. Using the balance sheet above, the $1,000 accounts payable must be paid within the period required (30, 60 or 90 days) depending on the credit terms offered.

It is important that a business uses their credit terms wisely. **Accounts payable** is an excellent source of short term finance. If a business uses its full credit period before paying its accounts payable then it has a valuable source of interest free finance. On the other side of the management coin, if it doesn't pay its debts within the credit period it risks losing its credit rating and reputation.

The management of loans is also important. Almost every business needs to borrow at some time in order to expand or purchase new capital and equipment. The areas that management must control closely are the debt to equity ratio i.e. the level of debt shouldn't exceed what is regarded as an acceptable level, which as discussed earlier shouldn't exceed 1:1 but in most cases should be less than this. The main danger here is that if interest rates increase greatly in a relatively short period of time then the business may not be able to maintain its repayments putting the business into a difficult cash flow situation and at great financial risk. The same would occur if the value of the assets decline.

Secondly, interest payments are a cost to the business and as such must be accounted for in the businesses overall budgeting. If the business finds itself in a difficult cash flow situation due to an unexpectedly low trading period, then it can renegotiate the loan- either the loan period or the terms of the loan i.e. the repayments.

Focus Point

An overdraft is an agreement between a bank and a business allowing the business to overdraw on its cheque account up to a certain, agreed figure.

Overdrafts are an excellent source of working capital. An overdraft is an agreement between a bank and a business allowing the business to overdraw on its cheque account up to a certain, agreed figure. They are in effect a credit limit, up to which a business can overdraw their accounts in order to purchase inventory or pay short-term debts. Where possible the business should aim to either reduce its overdraft or eliminate it altogether. In this way it is able to remove a liability. However, it is at least useful to maintain the overdraft facility for periods of low cash flow when the extra finance can be of great value to the business.

Strategies

There are a number of strategies for managing working capital.

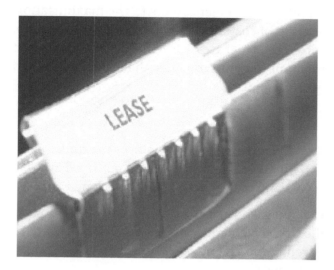

Leasing

This is an agreement whereby the owner of an asset (lessor) allows the use of an asset by a lessee for a periodic charge.

With capital equipment that is expensive or difficult to maintain, leasing is a valuable way of conserving working capital. Leasing saves the business an expensive up-front payment for expensive machinery or a fleet of cars, both of which will depreciate quickly and is a cost to the business. Even though lease payments are also a cost and a drain on working capital, they are a tax deduction to the business and that up-front payment doesn't have to be found.

Sale and lease back

This occurs where a business sells assets and leases them back from the purchaser. This then frees up capital that can be used for other purposes. This is becoming increasingly popular as a means of managing working capital. It has developed over recent years when large organisations such as banks and supermarkets realised that they had valuable assets tied up in real estate through their branch networks. These organisations sold their properties to investors who leased them back (as part of the deal) to those businesses. This freed up a great deal of working capital that could be used for other purposes.

Sale and lease back has had many excellent applications in other areas also. Many airline companies lease their aircraft in this way as do many hotel chains. Shipping companies do the same as do large companies with their vehicle fleets.

Profitability management

Effective profitability management refers to the maximisation of revenue and the minimisation of costs. This requires the business manager to constantly monitor the structure of revenues against the structure of costs. There are several management strategies that can be employed to manage the profitability of a business.

Cost control

Cost control refers to the concept of a business maximising its profits by minimising costs. Businesses must manage their fixed and variable costs, develop cost centres and practice cost minimisation.

One of the ways managers attempt to achieve this is to downsize their workforce. While this cost cutting strategy is still practiced, this trend has largely been discredited in recent years because of the ensuing loss of service provided by the business.

Other strategies used include the monitoring of inputs such as raw materials costs, transportation costs, costs of insurance or even power. In some cases the quality of raw materials was reduced as a means of reducing costs. In other cases prices would be increased in order to maintain profit margins.

In terms of fixed costs, there is very little that the business can do to reduce these costs. A fixed cost is a cost to a business that has to be made regardless of the level of output. Fixed costs include plant and machinery, insurance on premises or registration of motor vehicles. Senior management must try to obtain the most cost effective equipment in order to ensure that the business is not over stretched during levels of low production and consider leasing as opposed to purchasing.

Variable costs

Are costs that change according to the level of output. Variable costs may include labour costs or power bills which increase as production levels increase. The main way managers can reduce variable costs is through increased efficiency in the business. For example, by ensuring that the cheapest power sources are used and that the power is used efficiently. Staff training will also increase efficiency and therefore reduce costs. Finally, the adoption of Just In Time stock management in recent years has increased efficiency and therefore reduced variable costs.

Another strategy for profitability management is the establishment of cost centres within a business. A cost centre is a department, division or identifiable centre in a business where costs are incurred and monitored e.g. office administration. Staff involved in this unit are held responsible for all the costs incurred by that unit. In this way costs can be minimised. A cost centre report is devised by the personnel running that unit. The following example shows a cost centre report for an accounting department and the costs for which that department is responsible.

Cost Centre report of accounting department for a set period

Staff Costs	$13,000
Electricity	$200
Telephone	$300
Computer consumables	$400
Department Costs	$13,900

- The last area of cost control is that of **expense minimisation**. Expense minimisation is simply a concept of minimising expenses within a business. As discussed earlier, fixed costs such as wages and salaries could be minimised by downsizing or making the most efficient use of plant and equipment. With variable costs, managers can minimise costs through the expeditious use of variable inputs such as raw materials. During quiet trading periods or during times of economic down turn, expenses are minimised automatically if production declines.
- In order to minimise expenses it is essential for business to develop an expense budget. An expense budget lists all the activities of a business and the associated expenses involved. By carefully managing an expense budget, costs can be minimised by ensuring that expenses remain within that budget.

> **Focus Point**
>
> *A cost centre is a department, division or identifiable centre in a business where costs are incurred and monitored*

Revenue Controls

Revenue controls are aimed at maximising revenues received by the business through its business and financial activities. There are several types of revenue controls through the development of sales objectives, an appropriate sales mix and pricing policy.

Sales Objectives

Relate to the concept of increasing and maximising sales in order to maximise revenue. To do this sales targets must be set so that revenues can be maximised. These sales targets must be continually monitored to ensure that the sales effort is being maintained.

Sale Mix

The sales mix refers to the mix of the products produced and offered for sale by a business. Managers must monitor the sales mix in order to determine which products provide the greatest return. Products that are not returning sufficient revenue to the business will be considered for a greater marketing effort, improved efficiency of production or even deletion if it is deemed unlikely that the product can return sufficient revenue to that business. Obviously every product will not necessarily produce the same return, but each business will have its own parameters within which the product return should fall.

Pricing Policy

Finally, the pricing policy used by a business will help determine the revenue of the business. The business must decide whether it will reduce prices in order to sell more or increase prices and risk reduced sales. This decision will depend on the product and how much a price increase will affect the demand for that product.

The business can also use other pricing policies and marketing strategies such as discounts, favourable credit terms and extended payment periods to help maximise and control revenue. Discounts will encourage buyers. Favourable credit terms and extended payment periods will encourage those customers who want the product but feel that it is too costly to purchase and pay for up front.

Global financial management

Many businesses are either global or operate in a global environment. By this we mean that they are dealing and trading directly in the global market place or have exposure to the global environment via the internet. We have seen recent examples with customers buying and selling products on line rather than in a physical location such as a store. In this instance there are a number of things that can affect the business that trades globally such as exchange rates, interest rates, methods of international payment, hedging and derivatives. We will look at each of these in turn.

Exchange rates

When businesses only do business within Australia the concept of exchange rates is of no consequence. This is because the business is dealing in the one currency (Australian dollars) and a dollar is worth the same amount from Cairns to Perth and Darwin to Adelaide.

When companies become involved in international business, management needs to have a good knowledge of the international world of finance, which is not needed when marketing domestically. This results from the fact that each country has its own particular currency which is acceptable for domestic transactions, but which is unacceptable on international transactions. For example when an Australian exporter sends goods to Japan, the Australian business person wants to be paid in Australian dollars while at the same time the Japanese importer pays for the goods in Yen.

This it is necessary to convert Yen into Australian dollars so the Australian exporter can be paid. This is done through the foreign exchange market commonly known as the forex market. This is where the currencies of different countries are traded. In Australia the forex market operates through the Reserve Bank of Australia or other financial institutions which are authorised to buy and sell foreign currency on behalf of their clients.

Therefore, in order to pay for Australian goods in Japan, banks in Japan must hold Australian dollars. Likewise Australian banks (foreign exchange dealers) must hold Japanese Yen to pay for goods from Japan. When our forex dealers demand Japanese Yen to pay for Japanese goods, they pay for it in Australian dollars. Doing this increases the supply of our currency on the forex market.

When foreign exchange dealers are buying and selling each other's currencies, they must agree on a price. This price is the exchange rate i.e. the value of one currency against another.

The value of this currency constantly fluctuates according to the demand for that currency. If demand is high because overseas companies are buying our goods, then the value of the currency will go up and vice versa.

Companies involved in international business aren't always interested in exchange rates simply for trade reasons. Many companies borrow money from overseas and therefore must consider exchange rates very carefully, because the value of the Australian dollar, compared to the currency that is being borrowed, will affect the amount that has to be repaid.

For example, if an Australian business purchases goods worth $US1 million from a US company (the goods to be manufactured and delivered in 1 year) and they know that $A1.00 = $US 0.90, then they know that they will have to pay $A1.10 million for the goods when they are delivered. However if the value of the Australian dollar depreciates (falls) to say $US 0.50, during the year then they will have to pay $A2 million when the goods are delivered.

Now, it could be that the Australian dollar appreciates (rises) against the US dollar during the year (as happened in 2011) in which case the Australian purchaser pays back less than the $US1.10 million. In this case the Australian purchaser is happy, because they have received a better deal than expected. We will look at methods of protection against the risk of a falling dollar shortly.

International trade requires conversion from one currency to another.

Interest rates

Whether borrowing money domestically or internationally, the cost of borrowing is interest. High interest rates will attract foreign funds into Australia for investment purposes, increase the demand for Australian dollars and therefore push up its value. It will also have the effect of reducing demand for Australian exports because of the increased value of our dollar.

> **Focus Point**
>
> *Whether borrowing money domestically or internationally, the cost of borrowing is interest.*

Likewise, low interest rates will divert foreign funds from Australia, reduce the demand for the Australian dollar and depreciate its value. This will have the effect of increasing demand for Australian exports because of the lower valued dollar.

Looked at from another perspective, Australian business people will tend to borrow overseas when domestic interest rates are high and borrow at home when domestic interest rates are low.

Methods of international payment

We now turn our attention to the various methods of payment that are used in the world of global business. There are several ways that the international business person will pay for their goods.

Nothing beats **travelling to the markets** to which your company is exporting and meeting the customers and distributors. Many company's export sales are **insured for non-payment. EFIC** offers exporters insurance for exporters to cover 90% of the costs when a debtor defaults for payment periods longer than 180 days.

However **travelling to the market** provides the business person with first-hand knowledge of the customer and also allows the business person to seek new customers in the region while travelling. It must also be remembered that any overseas travel for business purposes can also be claimed for taxation purposes.

As discussed above, currency fluctuations can cause difficulties for businesses making payments for goods purchased from overseas. The business person should hedge against the risks of currency losses. (More will be said about this shortly)

Cash in advance. This is when an overseas buyer sends a remittance of money for payment for the goods at the time, or at some time before the goods are shipped. This is obviously the most satisfactory way of receiving payment as the Australian exporter has the money in the bank before the goods leave Australia.

Letter of credit. Another way to ensure payment is to organise a **letter of credit with a bank,** which arranges for a transfer of funds with the overseas customer's bank. As an exporters goods arrive at their destination, documents are exchanged and funds are immediately deposited in the exporter's account. This letter of credit states that the buyer is good for the money and will be paid on demand by the buyers bank.

There are two types of letters of credit---an irrevocable letter of credit and a revocable letter of credit. An irrevocable letter of credit cannot be cancelled or amended without the consent of the exporter. A revocable letter of credit can be altered or cancelled by the buyer at any time without the consent of the exporter.

Any form of credit has its risks and that is why an exporter (who often must extend open credit to a buyer to close a sale) should know the buyer well. The buyer could become insolvent or simply delay payment. Overseas governments may change or war and civil strife might interfere with payment.

Bill of exchange. This is a major money market instrument. It is an unconditional order in writing, addressed by one person to another, signed by the person giving it, requiring the person to whom it is addressed to pay on demand, or at a certain time in the future a sum of money.

There are two types of bills of exchange. The first is a D/P bill (documents against payment) which is drawn "at sight" and requires the bank to obtain payment before delivering the shipping documents to the buyer. In some countries, it is customary to delay payment on a sight bill until the arrival of the goods in port. However, at least the exporter will receive his/her money before the goods are delivered to the buyer.

The second is a D/A bill (documents against acceptance) which is drawn for payment within a specified period, for example 60 days after sight. In this case, the shipping documents are delivered to the buyer after his/her acceptance of the bill. The exporter is then relying on the creditworthiness of the buyer. In other words in this case the buyer has 60 days to pay once the shipped documents are delivered.

Barter. This is not a very common form of payment, but occurs when a business person trades with a country whose currency is very weak and not dealt on the foreign exchange markets. In this case there will be little demand for the currency of that country and therefore little money available to pay for the goods. In this case the Australian business person may offer to **barter** their goods for goods that will sell in Australia. In this way the two business people will overcome the exchange problems that exist.

- **Through an open account**: This is similar to the ordinary system of selling on credit on the domestic market. No bill of exchange is drawn up and the overseas buyer pays by remittance on receiving the goods, or a certain time afterwards. This method involves a considerable credit risk and is generally only used between firms of a long-standing connection.
- **Clean payment**: In clean payment method, all shipping documents, including title documents are handled directly between the trading partners. The role of banks is limited to clearing amounts as required. Clean payment method offers a relatively cheap and uncomplicated method of payment for both importers and exporters.

International factoring. This is a system where someone takes up your risk by buying out your contract. They buy the accounts receivable.

Summary of the rules with international payments

1. Make sure payments are guaranteed by taking out insurance or securing a letter of credit. Also, check the creditworthiness and reliability of overseas customers and distributers by visiting them and gathering information about their payment history.
2. It is dangerous to seek extra profit by gambling on currency fluctuations. Hedge against the risks of currency losses.
3. Try to obtain payment before the goods are shipped (cash in advance)
4. Obtain a letter of credit
5. Through a bill of exchange
6. By barter
7. Through an open account
8. Clean payment
9. Through international factoring

Hedging

As touched on earlier, if an Australian business orders goods from an American company, deliverable in say 12 months time and the value of the Australian dollar falls against the currency of the country from where the goods are being made, then the Australian business will have to pay more for those goods when they are delivered.

Now, it could very well be that the Australian dollar appreciates (rises) against the U.S. dollar during the year, in which case the Australian borrower pays <u>less</u> than they expected. In this case the Australian business person is happy because he/she has received a better deal than expected.

What is the Australian business person going to do to protect themselves against a depreciation of our currency against that of the US currency?

It must **hedge** its borrowings by arranging what is known as **forward cover**. The system works like this:

When the Australian business person contracts to buy the goods at today's prices i.e. $1,000,000 at $US0.70 this is the **current or spot rate**. In order to ensure they don't pay any more than they expect in 12 months time, they arrange **forward cover** on that money. That is the business person contracts with a bank or other financial agent to buy $US forward to the date they will receive and pay for the goods. In other words, the business person will establish another financial arrangement, this time a forward contract, by which it will require the financial agent to deliver to it in one years time an amount equivalent to the amount of money required for a price in Australian dollars agreed to <u>**now**</u> - <u>***at a price slightly above the spot rate***</u>. In this way the Australian business person is **insuring** against a possible depreciation of the Australian dollar over the period of the contract.

Sometimes the business person doesn't wish to physically buy the foreign currency (in this case U.S. dollars) instead they may choose to use another hedging tool through the **futures** market. In this case the business person uses what is known as the `**non-deliverable**` market as opposed to the physical market. In our example above the business person bought U.S. dollars on the physical or deliverable market as they really wished to have the funds transferred to their account to repay the U.S. dollar debt at the end of the year.

By using the **futures** market, the business person can still hold a square position and hedge against a depreciation of the Australian dollar (or appreciation of the U.S. dollar) by obtaining a forward contract for the period of concern, but specify that it was not for delivery i.e. no currency changes hands.

Another way of obtaining funds overseas at the most favourable rates of interest and at the same time protecting the amount that has to be repaid is by being involved in **swaps**. This form of hedging is fairly complicated, so it will be explained in its simplest terms.

Basically, **swaps** take place when two different countries agree to swap currencies so that one country can use the currency of the stronger country e.g. US dollars to purchase the goods and services and the stronger country hopes that the value of the currency of the weaker will appreciate as a result of improved economic fortunes so that a profit can be made on that currency when it is sold.

Exposure netting relates to portfolio investment. In this case a bank will try to maximise its position in the market. If it possesses financial products it looks to get a grasp of its position in the market and maximise its position financially.

Derivatives are simple financial contracts whose value is linked to or derived from an underlying asset, such as stocks, bonds, commodities, loans and exchange rates. They are international financial instruments for spreading risk or hedging using the same principle as above i.e. that they will appreciate in value. They include: futures, options, swaps, forward rate agreements.

The principal focuses of derivatives markets are currencies and interest rates. The turnover in the derivatives markets is now much larger than the cash markets. Only 1 per cent of the foreign exchange markets involves payment for trade. Most of it involves forms of derivatives trading. An important point to note is that the amount of foreign exchange traded in one day is equivalent of all the reserves of the world's central banks. This severely limits the ability of central banks to influence the flow of finance in the global economy and thus the impact those flows can have on a nation's exchange rate.

Trading in world currencies on derivative markets limits the capacity of central banks to influence exchange rates.

REVISION QUESTIONS 3.4

1. What is meant by the term "cash flow management"?

    _____

    _____

    _____

    _____

2. What is a cash flow statement and why is it regarded as a planning tool?

    _____

    _____

    _____

    _____

    _____

    _____

3. Explain the impact of the following terms on the maintenance of cash flow within a business.

    Distribution of Payments

    _____

    _____

    _____

    _____

    Discount for Early Payment

    _____

    _____

    _____

    _____

    Factoring

    _____

    _____

    _____

    _____

4. Define working capital and what do we mean by working capital management?

    _____

    _____

    _____

    _____

5. When managing working capital, the business must manage its current assets and its current liabilities. Explain how a business will exercise control over cash, receivables, inventories (assests), payables, loans and overdrafts.

    Cash

    _____

    _____

    _____

    _____

    Receivables

    _____

    _____

    _____

    _____

    Inventories

    _____

    _____

    _____

    _____

    Payables

    _____

    _____

    _____

    _____

Loans

_____

_____

_____

_____

Overdrafts

_____

_____

_____

_____

6. Name the two strategies for maintaining working capital and give an example of each.

1. _____

_____

_____

2. _____

_____

_____

_____

7. What is meant by the term profitability management?

_____

_____

_____

_____

_____

_____

REVIEW QUESTIONS 3.4 Page 4

8. When a business tries to manage its profitability it must look at its costs and revenues. Describe the concepts of fixed and variable costs, cost centres, expense minimisation and the concept of revenue controls.

_____

_____

_____

_____

_____

_____

_____

_____

_____

_____

_____

9. Explain the effects of exchange rates and interest rates on a business person who is selling their product on the global market compares with a business person who only trades domestically.

_____

_____

_____

_____

_____

_____

_____

_____

_____

_____

_____

_____

10. There are several methods of payment used by businesses when trading globally. Briefly explain each method.

Travel to markets

_____

_____

_____

_____

_____

Cash in advance

_____

_____

_____

_____

_____

Line of credit

_____

_____

_____

_____

_____

Bill of exchange

_____

_____

_____

_____

_____

Barter

_____

_____

_____

_____

_____

Open account

_____

_____

_____

_____

_____

Clean payment

_____

_____

_____

_____

_____

International factoring

_____

_____

_____

_____

_____

_____

11. What is hedging?

_____

_____

_____

_____

12. What are derivatives?

_____

_____

_____

_____

_____

PRACTICE SHORT ANSWER STYLE QUESTIONS

(N.B. These are simulation questions only and may not necessarily be similar to actual HSC short answer questions. Marks allocated are guides only)

Question 1 (10 marks)

You are interested in buying Hannah and Matthew's book shop located in a quiet part of a shopping centre.

Their accountant gives you the following financial information.

Current Assets		Current Liabilities	
Cash	6,500	Overdraft	12,000
Accounts Receivable	3,500	Accounts Payable	47,000
Inventories	20,000		
Non-Current Assets		**Owners Equity**	
Furniture & Fittings	5,300	Equity	4,000
Goodwill	28,000	Retained Profits	300

Marks

a. Describe ONE factor that you should consider before buying this business.　　2

_____

_____

_____

_____

_____

_____

_____

b. What is goodwill?　　2

_____

_____

_____

_____

_____

_____

    c. State and calculate a liquidity ratio for this business.   **2**

_____

_____

_____

_____

_____

_____

_____

    d. Suggest how this liquidity ratio might affect your decision
to buy this business.   **2**

_____

_____

_____

_____

_____

_____

_____

_____

_____

    e. Calculate and comment on this business's gearing ratio   **2**

_____

_____

_____

_____

_____

_____

_____

_____

_____

Question 2 (10 marks)

The management of Lembach and Associates has asked you to provide recommendations to assist their business. They have provided you with the following information.

Balance Sheet as at 30 Dec 2014

Assets		Liabilities	
Debtors	200,000	Creditors	180,000
Accts receivable	350,000	Overdraft	40,000
Buildings	615,000	Term Loan	50,000
		Owners Equity	
		Capital	160,000
		Retained profit	735,000
	_____		_____
	1,165,000		1,165,000

Additional information	$
Sales	1,000,000
Opening inventories	50,000
Purchases	200,000
Interest expense	15,000

Marks

a. State and calculate a liquidity ratio.   2

_____

_____

_____

_____

_____

b. State and calculate a profitability ratio.   2

_____

_____

_____

_____

_____

c. Identify two aspects of the Lembach & Associates Balance Sheet as of 31 Dec 2012 that would be of concern to a potential investor. 2

_____

_____

_____

_____

_____

_____

_____

_____

d. Outline two financial strategies to address the concerns that you identified in part (c) 4

_____

_____

_____

_____

_____

_____

_____

_____

_____

_____

_____

_____

_____

_____

_____

_____

_____

Question 3 (6 marks)

The CEO of Watt/Lembach and Associates, Mr Mike Lembach, has appointed you as financial advisor to their business. He has asked you to look at their balance sheet and help him with the following:

Balance Sheet of Lembach & Associates as of June 30 2014

Current Assets		Current Liabilities	
Cash	50,000	Creditors	70,000
Debtors	10,000	Overdraft	90,000
Inventories	20,000		
Non-Current Assets		**Non-Current Liabilities**	
Premises	400,000	Mortgage	250,000
Plant & Equipment	10,000	Bank Loan	60,000
Furniture & Fittings	50,000		
		Owners' Equity	
		Capital	30,000
		Net Profit	40,000
	540,000		540,000

a. Using an appropriate ratio, calculate the liquidity of this business.   2

_____

_____

_____

_____

b. Use ratio analysis to test the business for solvency. What is your conclusion? Explain why.   3

_____

_____

_____

_____

_____

c. As its financial advisor, what would you suggest it do?   3

_____

_____

_____

_____

Question 4 (8 marks)   Marks

1. Describe the difference between debt and equity financing   2

_____

_____

_____

_____

_____

_____

_____

_____

_____

2. Identify whether each of the following is a source of debt or equity and
    explain the meaning of each.   6

    a. Creditors

    _____

    _____

    _____

    _____

    _____

    b. Retained profits

    _____

    _____

    _____

    _____

    _____

    c. Bank overdraft

    _____

    _____

    _____

    _____

    _____

Question 5 (5 marks)

"The Business Cycle and Financial Markets are closely linked"

Marks

a. Give an example of a "financial institution" 1

_____

_____

_____

_____

_____

_____

b. Describe the role of the Australian Securities
Exchange (ASX) 4

_____

_____

_____

_____

_____

_____

_____

_____

_____

_____

_____

_____

_____

_____

_____

_____

_____

Question 6 (5 marks)

Selected Information for Mike's Beauty Parlour June 2014	
Owners Equity	**$**
Capital	60,000
Retained profits	20,000
Liabilities	
Current Liabilities	
Overdraft	2,000
Accounts payable	20,000
Term loan	10,000
Non-Current Liabilities	
Mortgage	30,000

Additional information:

	June 2012	June 2013
Gearing	3:1	2:1

Marks

a. Calculate and comment on the Gearing ratio for Lembach's beauty Parlour in 2014   2

_____

_____

_____

_____

b. Analyse the gearing trend for the past three years and comment on the financial management of this business.   3

_____

_____

_____

_____

_____

_____

_____

Question 7 (5 marks)

Lembach's Fine Wines			
Current Assets	**$**	**Current Liabilities**	**$**
Debtors	5,000	Accruals	-
Inventories	22,000	Creditors	20,000
Prepayments	500		
Cash	1,000		
Industry Averages:	Debt to Equity	2.1 : 1	
	Current Ratio	2.5 : 1	

Marks

a. Determine the level of working capital and calculate the working capital ratio for Lembach's Fine Wines.　　　2

_____

_____

_____

_____

_____

_____

_____

_____

b. With reference to actual items in the balance sheet, analyse the results obtained in (a) compared with the industry average.　　　3

_____

_____

_____

_____

_____

_____

_____

_____

_____

_____

8. List and define the five objectives of financial management   (10 marks)

_____

_____

_____

_____

_____

_____

_____

_____

9.

  a. Give an example of a "financial institution"   (1 mark)

_____

_____

_____

  b. Describe the role of the Australian Securities
     Exchange (ASX)   (4 marks)

_____

_____

_____

10. Mike is about to establish a business and needs to obtain finance to assist
his establishment. He is considering debt and equity finance and is unsure
of which to use.

  a. Describe one advantage and one disadvantage of
     debt finance   (2 marks)

_____

_____

_____

_____

  b. Describe one advantage and one disadvantage of
     equity finance   (2 marks)

_____

_____

_____

_____

_____

Glossary

Australian Securities and Investment Commission (ASIC): A government body established to monitor and regulate Australia's corporations, markets and financial services.

Australian Securities Exchange (ASX): The Australian Securities Exchange (ASX) provides a forum for businesses and individuals to buy and sell shares.

Awards: An award is an enforceable document containing minimum terms and conditions of employment in addition to any legislated minimum terms.

Balance Sheet: This statement gives a summary of the financial position of a business at a particular point in time. It shows the assets and liabilities of the business together with the value of owners equity in the business.

Banks: Secure organisation which uses funds deposited for investment by customers to provide cash and loans as required. Banks also exchange currencies and and provide a venue for financial transactions. As a group, banks are by far the largest financial providers in Australia.

Benchmarking refers to the establishment points of reference from which quality or excellence is measured.

Bills of exchange: (see commercial bills)

Budgets: Budgets are quantitative forecasts that help guide the use of the financial inputs and outgoings of a business.

Capital expenditure budget: A schedule setting out the planned expenditure on new machinery, buldings, plant and equipment.

Cash flow budget: A schedule of expected receipts and expenditure for a business. It differs from a cash flow statement, because it relates to future cash flows.

Cash flow statement: A cash flow statement is a summary of the movements of cash during a given period of time.

Certified Agreement: A certified agreement is an agreement made between employers and employees regarding wages and conditions in a workplace which has been ratified and approved by an appropriate tribunal or commission.

Commercial bills: These are known as bills of exchange. They are a form of short term (business) loan where a borrower agrees to repay a cash advance in 30 ,60 or 90 days as agreed.

Communication skills: Skills which enable people to understand each other. If a manager communicates effectively his plans will be followed and the business will grow.

Competitive positioning: Is about defining how you'll "differentiate" your offering and create value for your market.

Competitive pricing: This occurs when prices are set in relation to competitors prices.

Computer aided design (CAD): Design functions are automated by using computers.

Computer aided manufacture (CAM): This is software which allows the manufacturing process to become controlled by a computer.

Consumer markets: These consist of all the individuals and households who buy goods and services for personal consumption.

Contract manufacturing: The practice of outsourcing production instead of producing the function in house.

Contract worker: A contract worker hires his labour on an hourly basis, instead of becoming an employee.

Control: This is one of the managerial functions like planning, organizing, staffing and directing. In quality management, it is the operative stage, and may be used to describe all of these functions.

Corporate responsibility: The responsibility that business has to other businesses and the community generally.

Cost centre: A cost centre is a location, function or items of equipment monitored to determine operating costs for control purposes.

Cost control: Cost control involves careful purchasing, minimizing waste and efficient inventory control.

Cost leadership: This is an operating policy producing goods or services at the lowest cost possible to the business. Lower costs maximises profits, enabling business to establish a competitive advantage over its competitors.

Cost pricing: Selling goods at the producer's historical cost, i.e without making a profit.

Credit terms: These are the conditions of sale setting out how goods will be paid for, and the time to pay (30, 60 or 90 days).

Current assets: Consist of assets that can be turned into cash in a short period of time (usually within the accounting period). Current assets include cash, accounts receivable, inventories (which can be turned to cash quickly) and cash paid in advance.

Current liabilities: These are liabilities that may be called on in the short term (within one accounting period) and include accounts payable and overdrafts.

Customer orientation: When identifying consumer needs the marketer must identify what the consumer wants.

Customisation: Is the personalisation of products and services for individual customers.

Customise: To customise is to modify something according to a customer's individual requirements.

Data Miners: These are organisations which use huge data bases to pin point consumer preferences.

Debentures: A debenture is a loan to a company that is not necessarily secured by a mortgage on specific property but secured by the overall assets of the company.

Deceptive and misleading advertising: This occurs when, in the promotion of a product or service, a representation is made to the public that is false or misleading.

Demographics: Age, income, gender, marital status, sex, income etc

Derivatives: These are simple financial contracts whose value is linked to or derived from an underlying asset, such as stocks, bonds, commodities, loans and exchange rates.

De-skilling: This occurs when changed procedures (usually as a result of technology) removes a job that once required skill and replaces it with a job that doesn't.

Discounts: These are given on goods and services to encourage consumers to buy the product.

Discounts for early payments: Many businesses offer discounts to debtors for early payments as a means of improving cash flow.

Distribution channels: This covers the way in which a product is distributed from the factory to the consumer.

Double Loop learning: results in radical changes in the way the company does business. Double-loop learning allows the organisation to break out of existing thought patterns and to create a new mindset.

Effective profitability management: Refers to the maximisation of revenue and the minimisation of costs.

Efficiency: Describes how well a business is being run i.e. how efficiently the business is using its resources such as labour, finance or equipment.

e-marketing or electronic marketing: refers to the application of marketing principles and techniques via electronic media and more specifically the Internet.

Employees: People who work for employers for a wage or salary.

Employer associations: advise employers of their rights and obligations with regard to their employees and provide representation at Industrial Relations Commission (IRC) hearings where necessary.

Employers or management: is the group of people who own and manage a business.

Employment Contract: An employment contract is an agreement between an employer and employee/s that defines the rights and conditions for work.

Enterprise Agreement: An enterprise agreement is an agreement between an employer and an employee or employee group which covers wages and terms and conditions of work.

Equal Employment Opportunity (EEO): An employment policy where employees and employers have the responsibility to work to their full capacity, to recognise the skills and talents of other staff members to respect cultural and social diversity among colleagues and customers, to refuse to co-operate in, or condone any behaviour that may harass a colleague. (www.lawlink.nsw.gov.au)

Equity: Refers to the capital and accumulated funds and reserves shown in the balance sheet that is the owners share of a business.

Equity finance: The money (capital) put into a business by its owners. This may consist of cash, shares purchased in the business or retained profits. (See retained profits)

Exchange rate: i.e. the value of one currency against another.

Expense budgets: A forecast of all the activities of a business and the associated expenses involved.

Expense minimisation: A policy or practice of producing goods or services at the lowest possible cost or expenditure.

External funds: are the funds used in a business that have been obtained from a source outside the business. This is usually in the form of debt finance.

Factoring: This is the selling of accounts receivable to a financier. This is regarded as an important source of finance because the business is receiving immediate funds to use as working capital.

FIFO(First -In-First Out): An asset-management and valuation method in which the assets produced or acquired first are sold, used or disposed of first. FIFO may be used by a individual or a corporation.

Fixed cost: A fixed cost is a cost to a business that has to be made regardless of the level of output.

Flat Management Structures: As a response to change, flatter management structures have become more common over the past ten years. Businesses adopt a flatter management structure to reduce the number of levels of management, giving greater responsibility to middle managers.

Flexible employees: work flexible hours according to need. The conditions here are similar to casual employees unless a permanent employment agreement is decided on.

Flexible work practices: These are patterns of work that allow employees to vary their work commitments around the pressures of other responsibilities. They can assist employees in effectively managing work and family duties.

Foreign exchange (forex) market: The forex market is where currencies are traded by financial institutions acting as buyers and sellers.

Gantt chart: is a sequencing tool presented as a bar graph with time and activities shown on the two axes.

Global branding: This refers to the use of a brand name that is known world-wide.

Globalisation: Globalisation is the bringing together all of the world's economies for the purposes of trade and culture. It is the removing of barriers--trade barriers, language barriers, cultural barriers. It leads to the freeing up of the movement of labour from one country to another, the unification of laws and the unification of currency. It also involves financial flows, investment, technology and general economic behaviour in and between nations.

Global pricing: This is a contract between a customer and a supplier where the supplier agrees to charge the customer the same price for the delivery of parts or services anywhere in the world.

Global sourcing: This refers to the action of a business sourcing its raw materials from anywhere in the world. It is also a term used to describe the practice of sourcing raw materials from the global market for goods and services across geopolitical boundaries.

Goodwill: Goodwill is an intangible asset equal to that part of total assets which cannot be attributed to the separate business assets. In some ways it represents the synergy of the business.

Greenfields agreements: These involve a genuinely new enterprise that one or more employers are establishing or propose to establish and who have not yet employed persons necessary for the normal conduct of the enterprise. Such agreements may be either a single-enterprise agreement or a multi-enterprise agreement.

Growth: Business growth occurs with increased sales, by merging with other businesses or acquiring other businesses. In the balance sheet, growth is measured by the growth in the value of the business assets.

Head hunting: Recruitment by directly targeting a key individual who has the qualifications and characteristics that the firm is seeking. The prospect may already hold down a job in another business. The 'head hunter' usually makes an offer which, if accepted, enables the appointment to be made.

Historic cost: is the practice of valuing assets at the time of purchase.

Human Resource Management: This involves the use of qualified management staff in achieving the goals of the business, by ensuring that staff are productive, well-trained and satisfied in their jobs.

Implied conditions:

Consumers can expect the following when goods are sold:
1. the vendor is entitled to sell
2. the goods are unencumbered
3. the consumer has the right to quiet enjoyment
4. goods will comply with their description
5. goods will be of merchantable quality and fit for the purpose
6. goods will comply with a sample
7. services will be rendered with due care and skill
8. goods supplied with the service will be fit for purpose
9. services will be fit for the purpose.

Income statement: (see revenue/profit & loss statement)

Induction: This is the systematic introduction of new employees to their jobs, co-workers and the organisation. It may include on the job training.

Industrial markets: These are markets for goods and services which are used in the production of other goods and services and which are on sold to others in the production process.

Innovation: Innovation refers to the introduction of new systems, new technologies, approaches and products.

Inputs: These are the resources used in the process of production.

Intangibles: These are things such as patents, copyrights, trademarks and brand names and are often difficult to quantify.

Interest rates: are the price expressed as a percentage per annum for borrowing or lending money.

Intermediate goods: Those goods manufectered from raw materials and then used to make a finished product.

Intermediate markets: Often known as reseller markets. These markets consist of businesses that acquire goods for the purpose of reselling them to others in order to make a profit.

Internal sources of finance: are those funds provided to the business by its owners and are in the form of retained profits.

Interpersonal skills: Effective managers are be able to interact with their staff to enable the business to run smoothly. Skilful communication ensures tasks are perfomed efficiently and productively

Inventories: Inventories are raw materials, goods in transit and complete and incomplete work (work in progress). Inventories are expensive and can often comprise 50% of working capital

Job design: Job design determines the way work is organised and performed. The process identifies the work to be done, how the job will be done, the skills, knowledge and abilities (capabilities) needed to do the job and how the job contributes to achieving organisational goals.

Kaizen: This is the Japanese concept of constantly seeking improvement and questioning current methods of production.

Leadership style: The manner and approach of providing direction, implementing plans, and motivating people.

Leasing: This is an agreement whereby the owner of an asset (lessor) allows the use of an asset by a lessee for a periodic charge.

LIFO (last-in-first-out): An asset-management and valuation method that assumes that assets produced or acquired last are the ones that are used, sold or disposed of first.

Line management: Management of a business concerned with acquiring, producing and supplying goods and services to consumers. (Other management is involved in supporting line managers pursue these objectives. Human resource and administration managers would fall into this support function.)

Liquidity: is the ability of a business to pay its short term obligations as they fall due.

List pricing: This is the price a product is set at on a sellers' schedule. The list price is the normal selling price without discounts.

Logistics: Logistics is the internal and external transport,storage and distribution resources of a business

Long-term borrowing: These are regarded as borrowings that will take longer than a year to repay.

Loss leader: A loss leader is a product sold at a low price (at cost or below cost) to stimulate other profitable sales.

Maintenance of human resources: This is the "keeping" of human resources by providing them with benefits such as a safe working environment, good pay and a fair and equitable industrial setting in which to work.

Management: Management is the process of integrating all the available resources of the business to achieve the aims of the organisation.

Management Consultant: A management consultant is someone from outside the business who, for a fee will come in to advise the business about problems with systems and procedures that the business cannot solve on its own.

Management control system: This is a system which gathers and uses information to evaluate the performance of different parts of the business or resources

Marketing: The coordination of activities that determine the product, price promotion and place (the Four P's) for a product or service.

Marketing aim: To meet the objectives of a business by satisfying a customer's needs and wants

Market penetration: This is strength of sales and marketing of the business and its product compared to the total market size.

Market pricing: This occurs where a business prices their product according to what the business feels the market can pay.

Marketing concept: The marketing plan or strategy adopted by a business seeking to satisfy consumer demand.

Market research: Is the systematic collection and analysis of information and findings relating to a marketing situation faced by a company.

Market Share: Expressed as a percentage of the available market for the product. For example if the total market is 100%, the share held by company X might be 6.5%

Market share analysis: This analysis involves comparing the market share of the business with ones competition.

Mentoring: This is a situation where a more experienced (usually older) staff member is assigned to look after the progress of a new employee in the workplace.

Middle Management: The level of management between top management and other workers. There may be a number of levels in a large business. Middle levels are progressively being reduced as business seeks greater efficiency and empathy with its staff.

Minimum employment standards: These relate to the minimum conditions under which an employee can be employed.

Mortgage: This is a loan giving a bank first claim over specified assets such as land or buildings which are used as security.

Motivation: This refers to the energy, direction, purpose and effort displayed by people in their activities.

Multi-enterprise agreements: These involve two or more employers that are not all single interest employers. competitors.

New issues (shares): This occurs when a private or public company wishes to raise more capital and issues a new issue of shares.

Niche markets: are small, specialised markets catering for a small clientele.

Nominal exchange rate risks: This refers to the risk of losing money on international transactions as a result of changes in the exchange rate i.e. a depreciation of the Australian dollar or an appreciation of the currency of the country we are dealing with thus forcing us to take a loss on the transaction.

Non-current assets: These are those assets that are held for a long period of time (longer than the accounting period). Assets that cannot easily be converted into cash.

Non-current liabilities: These are held for a long period of time (usually several years) and include mortgages and long-term borrowings.

Observation: This is the gathering of data through the observation of people, activity or results.

Operations/management: Operations or operations management can be described as the allocation and maintenance of machinery and resources (for example raw materials and labour), productivity, quality, wastage and the introduction of new technologies that will combine to produce a good or service. Operations may also refer to a wider sphere of production such as assembly, batching, creative design and packaging. It is sometimes also referred to as production management.

Outsourcing: This is a situation whereby a business contracts certain work "out" to professionals such as lawyers and accountants.

Operational planning: Making decisions about which groups or departments will be responsible for carrying out the various elements of the strategic plan, deciding what needs to be done, when, by whom and at what cost.

Opinion leaders: are used to promote a product by promoting it in written form or verbally.

Ordinary shares: These are shares issued to investors in companies that entitle purchasers (holders) to a part ownership of the business.

Outsourcing: This is a situation whereby a business contracts certain work "out" to professionals such as lawyers and accountants.

Overdrafts: An overdraft is an agreement between a bank and a business allowing the business to overdraw on its cheque account up to a certain, agreed figure.

Owners equity: This consists of funds placed into the business by its owners. They can also be described as the assets that the business holds on behalf of the owners and includes shares and retained profits.

Part-time employees: Can be permanent except they work reduced hours. For example a part-time teacher may work two or three days a week.

Payment period: These periods vary according to the amount borrowed and for what purpose. Borrowings may be free of interest for short periods or attract interest for longer periods.

Penetration pricing: This involves charging a very low price initially to generate high volume sales and gain market share. It is used to establish customers that will be loyal to the product in the long term.

People Skills: Those skills associated with the management of employees through leadership, good communication and interest in employees ambitions and progress.

Performance management: or appraisal is the process of assessing the performance of employees against actual results and expectations of the manager.

Permanent employees: Employees who hold down a job with security of tenure. They receive benefits such as compulsory superannuation, holiday pay and sick leave.

Physical evidence: Is the material part of a service. In marketing it may be the tickets, brochures or advertising: the non-physical part may be the entertainment of the spectacle provided by the sport.

Place: The methods of distribution, storage and delivery that are used for the product.

Political and default risk: This risk is associated with countries which have unstable governments or those that have a difficult balance of payments situation.

Potential market: is the set of consumers who have some level of interest in a product.

Price: The cost of the product in the market place together with the methods of pricing used, discounts or credit terms used.

Price discrimination: This occurs when a seller charges different prices to different consumers for the same product.

Price points: These are points where the price of a product is at its optimum i.e. at the point where a retailer will sell most of their products for maximum profit.

Price skimming: This can be applied to a new product that is attractive and which has little or no competition. A high price can be charged initially, but can only be maintained over the short term because the high price will attract competitors into the market and the new competition will force the price downwards.

Primary research: This involves collecting raw data from scratch i.e. data that has not been published elsewhere.

Process layouts: These are configurations in which operations of a similar nature or function are grouped together.

Product: All the different goods and services that are offered to customers, the way they are packaged and the types of after sales service offered.

Product approach: The product approach revolves around the idea that if producers produced products and services, then consumers would want them.

Product differentiation: can be defined as the variation between a number of models of the same basic product e.g. a brand of washing machine with six available models.

Product positioning: This is a key aspect of the marketing mix. It's the image a product has in the mind of a consumer. Products can be positioned in the market according to price and quality, image, target market or its competition.

Profitability: This refers to the yield or profit a business receives in return for its productive effort.

Proliferation: When a product category contains many brands with minor differences.

Promotion: This is the technique of presenting a product or service to a customer in such a way that the customer will want to purchase that product or service.

Promotional pricing: This involves a temporary reduction in price on a number of products on offer designed to increase sales in the short term and give the retail outlet a boost.

Public relations: This is any form of letting the customer know that a product exists and can involve any of the promotional methods. Publicity may involve such things as testimonial letters, word of mouth information, spotters fees and sponsorships of special events and sporting teams.

Quality assurance: The QA manager's role is to count, measure and report on all aspects of operations to enable the line manager to direct and supervise. QA reports will highlight any deviation from planned or standard performance and suggest what corrective action needs to be taken.

Quality Circles: These comprise groups of skilled employees gathered together in a process that aims to better the quality of a product/service or procedure that will benefit a customer or the business by decreasing unnecessary costs.

Quality control: This can be defined as the management procedures that are put in place to check the suitability of raw materials, progress of production and product output to minimise reprocessing, seconds, wastage, costs, warranty claims and service problems.

Quality Expectations: see **Quality Assurance**

Quality management: This involves control, assurance and improvement. It is a continuously cyclical process calling on all the entrepreneurial flair, innovative skills, experience, people management skills, decision making skills, communication skills that a manager has.

Recruitment: This involves the ways in which employees are acquired for the firm.

Redundancy payments: When a worker is no longer needed in the business, he becomes redundant, and receives compensation for losing his job.

Relationship marketing: A marketing strategy relying on a personal relationship with customers.

Research and Development: refers to "creative work undertaken on a systematic basis in order to increase the stock of knowledge, including knowledge of man, culture and society, and the use of this stock of knowledge to devise new applications" (OECD).

Resignation: The voluntary action taken by an employee to leave an employer.

Resistance to change: The unwillingness of employees or managers to embrace new practices. The source of change may be new technology, new inventions, new ideas or new stakeholders.

Resource markets: Are those markets for commodities such as minerals, agricultural products, people looking for work (human resources) and financial resources.

Retained profits: These are the profits retained by the business and which have not been distributed to the owners/shareholders in the form of dividends.

Return on capital: This is the percentage of profit before or after tax compared to the value of capital (money) invested in the business.

Revenue controls: These are aimed at maximising revenues received by the business through its business and financial activities.

Revenue/Profit & Loss Statement: This statement provides a summary of the trading operations of a business for a given period of time (usually one month or a year).

Robotics: The use of robots or automation to streamline operations, often eliminating boring repetitive tasks.

Sale and lease back: A device used by business to sell assets and lease them back from the purchaser. This then frees up capital that can be used for other purposes.

Sales mix: This refers to the mix of the products produced and offered for sale by a business.

Sales objectives: These relate to the concept of increasing and maximising sales in order to maximise revenue.

Scanning and Learning: is a process of gathering, analysing, and dispensing business information for tactical (short term) or strategic (long term) purposes.

Scheduling: This involves the time taken to complete a particular job.

Secondary research: Data that is already in existence and usually collected by someone else for some other purpose.

Seconds: These are goods which have failed to meet the design or quality standards of the business.

Security: The charge given over an asset or assets which will be given over to a lender if the borrower defaults on a loan.

Short-term borrowing: This is made up of overdrafts and commercial bills and is normally used when the business requires finance for a relatively short time of up to a year or when the finance is required to assist with working capital.

Separation of human resources: This is the business term that describes the reduction of staff numbers for a variety of reasons, including retirement and redundancy (including voluntary and involuntary redundancy).

Sequencing: This involves placing tasks into an order so that an operation runs smoothly.

Sales promotion: Sales promotions may take several different forms. A trade fair such as a motor show, computer show, sports or leisure show is one form of sales promotion. The producer demonstrates his/her wares in an area set aside for that particular business while potential customers can walk by and observe the products on show.

Secondary Industry: The industrial sector of an economy dominated by the manufacture of finished products.

Secondary target market: This is the second most important market identified as a consumer group for the output of the business.

Self-managing: Employees in a self managed business work in an autonomous fashion without the need for constant supervision.

Situation analysis: A situation analysis is an assessment of a business's current position, e.g. its market share, profitability or competition

Stakeholders: Stakeholders are those people or institutions with an interest in a business in some way.

Strategic alliance: A strategic alliance occurs where two or more businesses work together to achieve a particular goal.

Strategic analysis: Strategic analysis is the examination of a business in the light of long term (3 to 5 years) goals and objectives. It will usually consider budgets, forecasts and prospects

Strategic planning: Strategic planning is long term planning (3 to 5 years).

Strategic thinking: This is the ability to think beyond the immediate tasks.

Target market: This is a section of the public to whom the producer aims his/her products and marketing campaigns.

Teamwork: The ability to work together. If the manager is a "team player" he will inspire teamwork in employees.

Training: This is the preparation of employees to undertake existing or new tasks proficiently.

Variable costs: Those costs only incurred when something is produced, such as direct labour or raw materials used. They vary directly with the volume of sales or production.

Vision: This is the ability of management to see where the business needs to go in the future and what is required to succeed. It is also the ability to see the "big picture" with regard to business direction.

Voluntary administration: This is a process under the Corporations Act. It allows a caretaker (the voluntary administrator) to take control of the affairs of a company while the directors are given a chance to propose a resolution of the company's financial problems to its creditors.

Voluntary separation and Involuntary separation: Voluntary separation occurs when an employee leaves of their own free will. Involuntary separation occurs when an employee loses their job as a result of an employer's action.